THE
DISADVANTAGES
OF BEING
EDUCATED

AND OTHER ESSAYS

THE WORKS OF
ALBERT JAY NOCK

The Myth of a Guilty Nation
Jefferson
A Journey Into Rabelais's France
A Journal of These Days
Our Enemy, The State
Free Speech and Plain Language
Henry George; An Essay
Memoirs of a Superfluous Man
On Doing the Right Thing, and Other Essays
The Book of Journeyman; Essays from the New Freeman
The Works of Francis Rabelais, 2 vols.
The Theory of Education in the United States
*A Journal of Forgotten Days
*Letters from Albert Jay Nock
*Snoring as a Fine Art and Twelve Other Essays
*Selected Letters of Albert Jay Nock
*The State of the Union

Mr. Nock wrote introductions to:
Forty Years of It, by Brand Whitlock
How Diplomats Make War, by Francis Neilson
The Selected Works of Artemus Ward, edited by Albert J. Nock
Man Versus the State, by Herbert Spencer
Meditations in Wall Street, by Henry Stanley Haskins

Mr. Nock contributed to:
The Freeman Book (Selections from the Eight Volumes of the
Freeman, 1920-24, compiled by B.W. Huebsch)

*Published posthumously

For information concerning availability of these works
in various editions, reprints, etc. contact:

THE NOCKIAN SOCIETY
42 Leathers Road, Fort Mitchell, Kentucky 41017

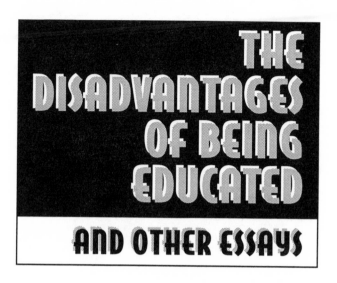

THE DISADVANTAGES OF BEING EDUCATED

AND OTHER ESSAYS

Albert
Jay
Nock

HALLBERG PUBLISHING CORPORATION

Nonfiction Book Publishers – ISBN 0-87319-041-6

Tampa, Florida 33623

ISBN Number 0-87319-041-6

Library of Congress Catalog Card Number 96-078216

Copyright © 1996 by Hallberg Publishing Corporation

All Rights Reserved

Cover design and typography by Michael X Marecek

Printed in the USA. First printing November 1996.
For information concerning Rights & Permissions or other questions
contact:

HALLBERG PUBLISHING CORPORATION
P.O. Box 23985 • Tampa, Florida 33623
Phone 1-800-633-7627 • Fax 1-800-253-READ

---·&·---

Dedicated to the furtherance of "the bond of joy"
through which "the called and chosen spirits
are kept together in this world."

---·&·---

CONTENTS

INTRODUCTION

A STROLL WITH ALBERT JAY NOCK

by Robert M. Thornton

Albert Jay Nock (1870-1945) was never a household name even in his own lifetime but his memory has been kept green in the half-century since his death. His *Jefferson* (1926), *Our Enemy, The State* (1935) and *Memoirs of a Superfluous Man* (1943), are still in-print and have never been long out-of-print. In fact, *Our Enemy, The State* and *Memoirs of a Superfluous Man* are, today, used as supplemental textbooks at major universities while Nock's *Jefferson* has been selected for sale to tourists visiting Monticello. In addition *Our Enemy, The State* has been translated and republished in Poland for use in their universities where concepts of limited government are virtually unknown. In 1991 Jacques Barzun wrote about the double please of reading Nock "for what he says and for the way he says it." Nock's work is "social and intellectual criticism at its best" and Barzun wrote optimistically that he "will surely climb in due course to his proper place in the American pantheon." Charles Hamilton noted that Nock "contributed some powerful and lasting criticism of the state of humane life in America." Nock was not a voluminous writer, wrote his friend, Frank Chodorov, but "had a rare gift of editing his ideas so that he wrote only when he had something to say and he said it with dispatch." Hendrik Willem van Loon exclaimed that Nock was "possessed of a rare genius for the handling of words." And finally, H. L. Mencken, no slouch himself as a prose stylist, declared that Nock "thinks in charming rhythm. There is never any cacophony in his sentences as there is never any muddling in his ideas. It is accurate, it is well ordered, and above all, it is charming."

Albert Jay Nock was not a reformer and found offensive any society with a "monstrous itch for changing people." He had "a great horror of every attempt to change anybody; or I should rather say, every *wish* to change anybody; for that is the important thing." Whenever one "*wishes* to change anybody, one becomes like the socialists, vegetarians, prohibitionists; and this, as Rabelais says, 'is a terrible thing to think upon.'" The only thing we can do to improve society, he declared, "is to present society with *one improved unit.*" Let each person direct his efforts at himself, no others; or as Voltaire put it "If faut cultiver notre jardin."

Nock knew very well that he was rowing against the tide and that his words would have no immediate effect on the course of human events but since his devotion was to the truth, he worried not at all about being out of step with his times. So why, then, did he bother to write at all? The "general reason" is that "when in any department of thought a person has, or thinks he has, a view of the plain intelligible order of things, it is proper that he should record that view publicly, with no thought whatever of the practical consequences, or lack of consequences, likely to ensure upon his so doing." He should not "crusade or propagandize for his view or seek to impose it on anyone . . ." The "special reason has to do with the fact that in very civilization . . . however addicted to the short-time point of view on human affairs, there are always certain alien spirits who . . . still keep a disinterested regard for the plain intelligible law of things, irrespective of any practical end." It was for them Nock wrote and them alone.

"Criticism's business," wrote Nock, "is with the past — especially the immediate past; concern with the present is the function of journalism." Critics have no business fumbling at what goes on in their time. They can make no judgement that is worth anything and neglect many good values that lie behind them. Goethe, the greatest of critics, said earnestly, "Don't read your fellow-strivers, fellow-workers."

The great critics, wrote Nock, help "the truth along *without encumbering it with themselves*." So much social criticism must be taken in small doses or one will come away depressed and generally in a mood to chuck it all. The reader may agree with everything the critics say, one hundred per cent, but he is nevertheless left in a despondent mood. Not so with the greatest critics who are aware "that for life to be fruitful, life must be felt as a joy; that it is by the bond of joy, not of happiness or pleasure, not of duty or responsibility, that the called and chosen spirits are kept together."

A civilized society, wrote Albert Jay Nock, is one which organizes a full collective expression of mankind's five fundamental social instincts:

- The instincts of workmanship (or, as he called it elsewhere, expansion and acquisition);
- of intellect and knowledge;
- of religion and morals;
- of beauty and poetry;
- of social life and manners.

When societies have gone on the rocks, "it was invariably the collective over-stress on one or more of these fundamental instincts that wrecked them." American society, he wrote from Brussels in 1931, is trying to force the whole current of our being through the narrow channel set by one instinct only: the instinct of acquisition and expansion. A society that give play to only this instinct "must inevitably be characterized by a low type of intellect, a grotesque type of religion, a factitious type of morals, an imperfect type of beauty, and imperfect type of social life and manners. In a word, it is uncivilized."

The trouble with our civilization, declared Nock, is that it makes such limited demands on the human spirit and the qualities that are distinctly and properly humane. We have been trying to live my mechanics alone, the mechanics of pedagogy, politics, industry and commerce. Instead of experiencing a change of heart, we bend our wits to devise changes in mechanics. But, continued Nock, "a nation's life consisteth not in the abundance of the things that it possesseth; that it is the spirit and manners of a people, and not the bewildering multiplicity of its social mechanisms that determine the quality of its civilization."

The sort of people Nock admired were those he found himself among many years ago in New England. Writing in 1930, he observed that "they like to work, and they are prosperous but they refuse to be dominated by heir business" and "resent an over-big rush of trade as keenly as the rest of America grabs for it, and cajoles and lies and grovels for it." Nock felt privileged "to sojourn among such people" and had "enormous admiration for their independence, self-respect and insight into the real values of life."

"If we look beneath the surface of our public affairs," wrote Albert Jay Nock in 1935, "we can discern one fundamental fact, namely: a great redistribution of power between society and State." All the various government activities "come to the same thing: which is, an increase of State power and a corresponding decrease of social power." This came about because "instead of recognizing the State as 'the common enemy of all well-disposed, industrious and decent men,' the run of mankind, with rare exceptions, regards it not only as a final and indispensable entity, but also as, in the main beneficent." Many people took for granted "that the citizen exists for the State, not the State for the citizen; that the individual has no rights which the State is bound to respect; that all rights are State-created," and "that personal government is quite consistent with democracy . . ."

Social power means the power generated and exercised by individuals and groups of individuals working in an economy which is free of government interference — an economy of free contract, "a system of voluntary cooperation." State power, on the contrary, means government going beyond its legitimate functions to enforce positive interventions upon the individual. Government intervention "on the individual should be purely negative in character. It should attend to national defense, safeguard the individual in his civil rights, maintain outward order and decency, enforce the obligations of contract, punish crimes belonging in the order of *malum in se* (evil in itself e.g. murder, theft) and make justice cheap and easily available." Nock was then, an enemy of the State but not an anarchist. His point was that "if the State were limited to purely *negative* interventions which I enumerated, and had no oversize power beyond that, then it wouldn't be the State anymore. It would then be *government* only . . ."

Years after Nock wrote about the State, more and more people are coming to realize with him that it is not the "proper agency for social welfare, and never will be, for exactly the same reason that an ivory paper-knife is nothing to shave with." The interest of society and the State are entirely different. Society gets on best when people are freest to do as they please so their interest is in "having as little government as possible and keeping it decentralized as possible." The State, of course, wants to have as much government as possible and to keep it highly centralized.

"Let us suppose," wrote Nock, "that instead of being slow, extravagant, inefficient, wasteful, unadaptive, stupid, and at least by tendency corrupt" the State changes its character and becomes infinitely wise, good, disinterested and efficient. Suppose it solves every individual problem and protects persons from every consequence of bad judgement, weakness or incompetence? Then, asked Nock, "what sort of person is the individual likely to become under those circumstances?" We have it, then, that "the worst of this ever-growing cancer of Statism is its moral effect." The moral judgement of the individual is weakened, wrote Nock, "as the State assumes more and more responsibility, offering cradle to grave 'security'."

In 1932 Albert Jay Nock wrote that since the turn of the century schools in The United States had been operating on an unsound theory of education. Put briefly, this theory declares that everyone can be educated, that everyone should be educated, and that an educated citizenry will make us a better nation. Nock believed that it was futile trying to translate this bad theory into good practice and that we were mistaken to think that a "general faith in machinery (was) an effective substitute for thought."

In 1970 Jacques Barzun wrote that "Nock's book on education (*The Theory of Education in the United States*, 1932) could have saved us endless mistakes had we heeded it during the past half century." Certainly what Nock said over sixty years ago has been proven correct by the failure to improve our schools despite numerous experiments and Federal "Aid-to-Education" programs that have spent billions of dollars in the past four decades. However well-intentioned, we have engaged in mere tinkering instead of being radical — that is, going deep to correct the problem instead of being concerned with the superficial.

The theory that our schools have been acting upon for nearly a century collapses if the first part — everyone is educable — is wrong. If everyone is not educable, then it makes no sense to say that everyone should be educated or that an educated citizenry will make us a better nation. Unfortunately, however, we have acted as if the theory is sound and to insure that everyone is "educated" the government makes attendance and tax support compulsory. This had led to many problems and the only solution is for attendance at schools and support of schools be as voluntary as attendance at and support of churches.

The theory of education in this country *is* wrong, declared Nock, because while nearly all of us can be trained to do something, not all of us are educable. This is not some obnoxious form of elitism anymore than is an acknowledgment that few can play basketball as well as Michael Jordan or the flute as well as James Galway. "It can not be too often reiterated that education is a process contemplating intelligence and wisdom, and employing formative knowledge for its purposes; while training is a process contemplating sagacity and cleverness, and employing instrumental knowledge for its purposes." Training has to do with earning a living; education has to do with preparation for living.

The educated man or woman, explained Nock, has the "power of distinterested reflection" by which he meant the "ability to take a detached, impersonal and competent view of something that deeply engages his affections, one way or other — something that he likes very much." Educated men and women, wrote Nock, are "capable of maintaining a mature and informed disinterestedness, a humane and elevated serenity in all their views of human life." They tend to "see things as they are." The best way to acquire this cast of mind is by way of the "grand old fortifying curriculum" the classical studies which used to be at the heart of a liberal arts education before schools became cafeterias of sort with the ever-growing selection of electives which even sixty years ago boggled the mind. Nock observed that "the literatures of Greece and Rome comprise the longest and fullest continuous record available to us, of what the human mind has been busy about in practically every department, I think, except music." The mind that has "attentively canvassed this record is not only a disciplined mind but an *experienced* mind; a mind that instinctively views any contemporary phenomenon from the vantage point of an immensely long perspective . . ."

Nock was once offered the chance to be head of the department of English literature by the president of a huge, sprawling, Mid-Western State university. "I told him I had not the faintest idea of how to set about it; I should be utterly helpless. All I could do would be to point to the university's library, and say — There it is — wade in and help yourselves." A flip response, some might say, but it got across Nock's belief that education is not a matter of someone pouring knowledge into another's brain and that the responsibility does not lie with the teacher. The student must shoulder the burden of learning with the teacher around only to help him along the way by asking a few questions or clearing away some difficulties. The root meaning of educate is, after all, to draw out, not to stuff in. So, as Nock put it, you cannot, in a sense, teach anyone anything but you can "l'arn him" something.

Speaking at Hillsdale College in 1994, Supreme Court Justice Clarence Thomas gave a powerful message about the importance of education for a black person coming from a background of poverty and prejudice. "I must first admit," declared Justice Thomas, "that I am somewhat old-fashioned about education. I opposed the move away from the old core requirements and traditional liberal arts education, and I still hold tenaciously to that position." Liberal arts education, he said, "was a way of showing us that we were to discipline, train, and expand our minds. It provided fewer opportunities to justify intellectual laziness and almost no opportunity to avoid some of the more difficult courses." It was the study of liberal arts that pulled him back "from the abyss of self destruction," and taught him to "confront and debate difficult ideas in a calm civil way." Education, said Justice Thomas, "most certainly gives us the means by which to earn a living, but it also provides the means to learn how to live."

The "Great Tradition" Nock wrote about years ago still lives!

"It is surely a fair question," wrote Nock, "whether a competent practice of religion calls for quite so much apparatus; metaphysical and physical, as the main body of organized Christianity has constructed and is trying, none too successfully, to keep in running order." Nock was convinced that Christianity was in its nature, incapable of being successfully organized or institutionalized. He found no evidence that Jesus ever contemplated either because his teaching seems to have been purely individualistic in its content. "In a word, it came to this: that if every *one* would reform *one* (that is to say, oneself) and keep *one* steadfastly following the way of life which He recommended, the Kingdom of Heaven would be coextensive with human society."

Of greatest importance, then, was the spirit of Christianity, not all the trappings of ecclesiastic religion. Religion, he declared, "is a temper, a frame of mind; the fruit of the Spirit, as St. Paul says, love, joy, peace, long-suffering, gentleness, goodness, faith, meekness, self-control." Nock did not find "any evidence that Jesus laid down any basic doctrine beyond that of a universal loving God and a universal brotherhood of man." He "exhibited a way of life to be pursued purely for its own sake, with no hope of any reward but the joy of pursuing it . . ."

Nock would have agreed with the esteemed Anglican, Dean (of St. Paul's) William R. Inge (1860-1954) who in 1953 wrote that "Old age has made me a better Christian and I fear a worse Churchman." Dean Inge believed that the time may come when nothing will be left of Christianity except the Christ-Mysticism of St. Paul and the law of love. He believed the Gospel of Jesus was a free personal piety, without any tendency towards the creating of a religious community. There has been a change in our time from authority to experience and mysticism has no tendency to form organizations. The Dean hoped it would take the place of the external props which St. Paul warned would "vanish away."

"The only apologetic for Jesus's teaching that I find in any way reasonable is the one which Jesus Himself propounded — experience." That is, His way of life was to be followed because experience will prove it is the best way. It was the signal merit of the Cambridge Platonists,[1] declared Nock, that they recognized experience as the sum-total of Jesus's own apologetic. Nock wrote:

> When *Smith* amplifies Luther's definition by saying, "Where we find wisdom, justice, loveliness, goodness, love, and glory in their highest elevations and most unbounded dimensions, that is He; and where we find any true participations of these, there is a true communication of god; and a defection from these is the essence of sin and the foundation of hell," — when Smith says this, one feels that he has gone as far with a prescriptive system of dogmatic theology as it is safe to go; and he goes no farther. *Taylor* also, with his mind on metaphysical credenda, gives warning that "too many scholars have lived upon air and empty nothings, and being very wise about things that are not and work not." *And work not* — there he comes back, as these men are always coming back, to the basic ground of practice, of conduct; and how great is the reason why they should, for as *Whichcote* says, "men have an itch rather to make religion than to practice it."

The teachings of Jesus may have been simple but the way of life He prescribed is an extremely arduous business which few are able to do. Jesus appears to have been clearly aware that this would be so but he was not offering an impracticable counsel of perfection. It has been done in "an inconspicuous way by incon-

---

[1]Among others, John Smith (1618-1652), Jeremy Taylor (1613-1667) and Benjamin Whichcote (1609-1683).

spicuous person, yet also by some like St. Francis and others among the great names one meets in the history of Christian mysticism, who circumstances rendered more or less conspicuous . . ."

POSTSCRIPT

Albert Jay Nock began his writing career in 1908 and until his death in 1945 wrote for several magazines, most frequently; American Magazine, Atlantic Monthly, Harper's, Scribner's and the American Mercury. He was co-editor of the Freeman (1920-1924) and wrote many pieces for that periodical which was "widely recognized as one of the best of American journalism."

Nock's first book was a collection of Freeman articles entitled *The Myth of a Guilty Nation* (1922). In the next two decades he published *Jefferson*** (1926), *On Doing the Right Thing and Other Essays* (1928), *Francis Rabelais: The Man and His Work* (1929), *The Book of Journeyman; Essays from the new Freeman* (1930), *The Theory of Education in the United States* (1932), *A Journey into Rabelais's France* (1934), *A Journal of these Days* (1934), *Our Enemy, The State*** (1935), *Free Speech and Plain Language* (1937), *Henry George; An Essay* (1939), and *Memoirs of a Superfluous Man*** (1943).

Published posthumously were: *Journal of Forgotten Days* (1948), *Letters from Albert Jay Nock* (1949), *Snoring as a Fine Art and Twelve Other Essays* (1958), *Selected Letters of Albert Jay Nock* (1962) and *The State of the Union** (1991).

Cogitations*, a collection of quotations gleaned from the writings of Albert Jay Nock, was published in 1970.

The titles marked with an asterisk are available from The Nockian Society, 42 Leathers Road, Fort Mitchell, Kentucky 41017. Those marked with a double asterisk are also available from the publisher, HALLBERG PUBLISHING CORPORATION, P.O. BOX 23985, TAMPA, FLORIDA 33623.

Robert M. Thornton is a retired businessman living in Fort Mitchell, Kentucky.

Full of this idea, I rushed into print with the suggestion that in addition to our present system of schools, colleges and universities which are doing first-class work as training schools, we ought to have a few educational institutions.

The Disadvantages of Being Educated

My interest in education had been comfortably asleep since my late youth, when circumstances waked it up again about six years ago. I then discovered that in the meantime our educational system had changed its aim. It was no longer driving at the same thing as formerly, and no longer contemplated the same kind of product. When I examined it I was as far "out" on what I expected to find as if I had gone back to one of the sawmills familiar to my boyhood in Michigan, and found it turning out boots and shoes.

The difference seemed to be that while education was still spoken of as a "preparation for life," the preparation was of a kind which bore less directly on intellect and character than in former times, and more directly on proficiency. It aimed at what we used to call training rather than education; and it not only did very little with education, but seemed to assume that training was education, thus overriding a distinction that formerly was quite clear. Forty years ago a man trained to proficiency in anything was respected accordingly, but was not regarded as an educated man, or "just as good," on the strength of it. A trained mechanic, banker, dentist or man of business got all due credit for his proficiency, but his education, if he had any, lay behind that and was not confused with it. His training, in a word, bore directly upon what he could do or get, while his education bore directly on neither; it bore upon what he could become and be.

Curiosity led me to look into the matter a little more closely, and my observations confirmed the impression that the distinction between training and education was practically wiped out. I noticed, too, that there was a good deal of complaint about this: even professional educators, many of them, were dissatisfied with it. Their complaints, when boiled down, seemed to be that education is too little regarded as an end in itself, and that most of the country's student population take a too strictly vocational view of what they are doing, while the remainder look at it as a social experience, encouraged largely in order to keep the cubs from being underfoot at home, and reciprocally appreciated mostly because it puts off the evil day when they must go to work; and that our institutions show too much complacency in accommodating themselves to these views.

These complaints, I observed, were not confined to educators; one heard them from laymen as well, and the laymen seemed to be as clear in their minds about the difference between education and training as the professional educators were. For example, one of America's most distinguished artists (whom I am not authorized to quote, and I, therefore, call him Richard Roe) told a friend of mine that when his ship came in he proposed to give magnificent endowments to Columbia, Harvard, Princeton and Yale on the sole condition that they should shut up shop and go out of business forever. Then he proposed to put up a bronze plate over the main entrance to each of these institutions, bearing this legend:

CLOSED
THROUGH THE BENEFACTION
OF
RICHARD ROE
AN HUMBLE PAINTER
IN BEHALF OF EDUCATION

As I saw the situation at the moment, these complaints seemed reasonable. Training is excellent, it can not be too well done, and opportunity for it can not be too cheap and abundant. Probably a glorified crèche for delayed adolescents here and there is a good thing, too; no great harm in it anyway. Yet it struck me as apparently it struck others, that there should also be a little education going on. Something should be done to mature the national resources of intellect and character as well as the resources of proficiency; and, moreover, something should be done to rehabilitate a respect for these resources as a social asset. Full of this idea, I rushed into print with the suggestion that in addition to our present system of schools, colleges and universities which are doing first-class work as training schools, we ought to have a few educational institutions. My notion was that the educable person ought to have something like an even chance with the ineducable, because he is socially useful. I thought that even a society composed of well trained ineducables might be improved by having a handful of educated persons sifted around in it every now and then. I, therefore, offered the suggestion, which did not seem exorbitant, that in a population of a hundred and twenty odd million there should be at least one set of institutions, consisting of a grade-school, a secondary school and an undergraduate college, which should be strictly and rigorously educational, kept in perpetual quarantine against the contagion of training.

II

This was five years ago, and about eighteen months ago I repeated the suggestion. My modest proposal was hardly in print before I received a letter from a friend in the University of Oxford, propounding a point which believe it or not — had never occurred to me.

> But think of the poor devils who shall have gone through your mill! It seems a cold-blooded thing . . . to turn out a lot of people who simply can't live at home. Vivisection is

nothing to it. As I understand your scheme, you are planning to breed a batch of cultivated, sensitive beings who would all die six months after they were exposed to your actual civilization. This is not Oxford's superciliousness, I assure you, for things nowadays are precious little better with us. I agree that such people are the salt of the earth, and England used to make some kind of place for them . . . But now — well, I hardly know. It seems as though some parts of the earth were jolly well salt-proof. The salt melts and disappears, and nothing comes of it.

As I say, I had never thought of that. It had never occurred to me that there might be disadvantages in being educated. I saw at once where my mistake lay. I had been looking at the matter from the point of view of an elderly person to whom such education as he had was just so much clear gain, not from the point of view of a youth who is about to make his start in the world. I saw at once that circumstances, which had been more or less in favour of my educated contemporaries, were all dead against the educated youngster of today. Therefore, last year, when I was appointed to deal again with the subject in a public way, I went back on all I had said, and ate my ration of humble-pie with the best grace I could muster.

Every shift in the social order, however slight, puts certain classes irrevocably out of luck, as our vulgarism goes. At the beginning of the sixteenth century the French feudal nobility were out of luck. They could do nothing about it, nobody could do anything about it, they were simply out of luck. Since the middle of the last century, monarchs and a hereditary aristocracy are out of luck. The Zeitgeist seems always arbitrarily to be picking out one or another social institution, breathing on it with the devouring breath of a dragon; it decays and dissolves, and those who represent it are out of luck. Up to a few years ago an educated person, even in the United States, was not wholly out of luck; since then, however, an educated young man's chance, or an educated young woman's, is slim. I do not here refer exclusively to the mere matter of picking up a living, although, as I shall show, education is a good bit of hindrance even to that; but also to conditions which make any sort of living enjoyable and worth while.

So in regard to my championship of education it turned out again that everybody is wiser than anybody, at least from the short-time point of view, which is the one that human society invariably takes. Some philosophers think that society is an organism, moving instinctively always towards the immediate good thing, as certain blind worms of a very low order of sensibility move towards food. From the long-time point of view, this may often be a bad thing for the worm; it may get itself stepped on or run over or picked up by a boy looking for fish-bait. Nothing can be done about it, however, for the worm's instinct works that way and, according to these philosophers, so does society's, and the individual member of society has little practical choice but to go along.

Hence our institutions which profess and call themselves educational, have probably done the right thing — the immediate right thing, at any rate — in converting themselves, as our drugstores have done, into something that corresponds only very loosely to their profession. No doubt the lay and professional complaint against this tendency is wrong; no doubt the artist Richard Roe's proposal to close up our four great training schools is wrong. No doubt, too, our young people are right in instinctively going at education, in the traditional sense of the term, with very long teeth. If I were in their place, I now think I should do as they do; and since I am in the way of recantation, as an old offender who has at last seen the light of grace, I may be allowed to say why I should do so — to show what I now plainly see to be the disadvantages of being educated.

III

Education deprives a young person of one of his most precious possessions, the sense of cooperation with his fellows. He is like a pacifist in 1917, alone in spirit — a depressing situation, and especially, almost unbearably, depressing to youth. "After all," says Dumas's hero, "man is man's brother," and youth especially needs a free play of the fraternal sense; it needs the stimulus and support of association in common endeavour. The survivor of an older generation in America has had these benefits in some degree; he is more or less established and matured and can rub along fairly comfortably on his spiritual accumulations; and besides, as age comes on, emotions weaken and sensitiveness is dulled. In his day, from the spiritual and social point of view, one could afford to be educated — barely and with difficulty afford it perhaps, but education was not a flat liability. It netted enough to be worth its price. At present one can afford only to be trained. The young person's fellows are turning all their energy into a single narrow channel of interest; they have set the whole current of their being in one direction. Education is all against his doing that, while training is all for it; hence training puts him in step with his fellows, while education tends to leave him a solitary figure, spiritually disqualified.

For these reasons: education, in the first place, discloses other channels of interest and makes them look inviting. In the second place, it gives rise to the view that the interest which absorbs his fellows is not worth mortgaging one's whole self, body, mind and spirit, to carry on. In the third place, it shows what sort of people one's fellows inevitably become, through their exclusive absorption in this one interest, and makes it hard to reconcile oneself to the thought of becoming like them. Training, on the other hand, raises no such disturbances; it lets one go on one's chosen way, with no uncertainty, no loss of confidence, as a man of the crowd. Education is divisive, separatist; training induces the exhilarating sense that one is doing with others what others do and thinking the thoughts that others think.

Education, in a word, leads a person on to ask a great deal more from life than life, as at present organized, is willing to give him; and it begets dissatisfaction with the rewards that life holds out. Training tends to satisfy him with very moderate and simple returns. A good income, a home and family, the usual run of comforts and conveniences, diversions addressed only to the competitive or sporting spirit or else to raw sensation — training not only makes directly for getting these, but also for an inert and comfortable contentment with them. Well, these are all that our present society has to offer, so it is undeniably the best thing all round to keep people satisfied with them, which training does, and not to inject a subversive influence, like education, into this easy complacency. Politicians understand this — it is their business to understand it — and hence they hold up "a chicken in every pot and two cars in every garage" as a satisfying social ideal. But the mischief of education is its exorbitance. The educated lad may like stewed chicken and motorcars as well as anybody, but his education has bred a liking for other things too, things that the society around him does not care for and will not countenance. It has bred tastes which society resents as culpably luxurious, and will not connive at gratifying. Paraphrasing the old saying, education sends him out to shift for himself with a champagne appetite amidst a gin-guzzling society.

Training, on the other hand, breeds no such tastes; it keeps him so well content with synthetic gin that a mention of champagne merely causes him to make a wry face. Not long ago I met a young acquaintance from the Middle West who has done well by himself in a business way and is fairly rich. He looked jaded and seedy, evidently from overwork, and as I was headed for Munich at the moment, I suggested he should take a holiday and go along. He replied, "Why, I couldn't sell anything in Munich — I'm a business man." For a moment or two I was rather taken aback by his attitude, but I presently recognized it as the characteristic attitude of trained proficiency, and I saw that as things are it was right. Training had kept his demands on life down to a strictly rudimentary order and never tended to muddle up their clear simplicity or shift their direction. Education would have done both; he was lucky to have had none.

It may be plainly seen, I think, that in speaking as he did, my friend enjoyed the sustaining sense of cooperation with his fellows. In his intense concentration, his singleness of purpose, and in the extremely primitive simplicity of his desires and satisfactions, he was completely in the essential movement of the society surrounding him; indeed, if his health and strength hold out, he may yet become one of those representative men like Mr. Ford, the late Mr. Eastman or Mr. Hoover, who take their tone from society in the first instance and in turn give back that tone with interest. Ever since the first westward emigration from the Atlantic seaboard, American civilization may be summed up as a free-for-all scuffle to get rich quickly and by any means. In so far as a person was prepared to accept the terms of this free-for-all and engage in it, so far he was sustained by the exhilaration of what Mr. Dooley called "th' common impulse fr th' same money." In so far as he was not so prepared, he was deprived of this encouragement.

To mark the tendency of education in these circumstances, we need consider but one piece of testimony. The late Charles Francis Adams was an educated man who overlived the very fag-end of the period when an American youth could afford, more or less hardly, to be educated. He was a man of large affairs, in close relations with those whom the clear consenting voice of American society acclaimed as its representative men, and whose ideals of life were acclaimed as adequate and satisfying; they were the Fords, Eastmans, Owen Youngs, Hoovers, of the period. At the close of his career he wrote this:

> As I approach the end, I am more than a little puzzled to account for the instances I have seen of business success — money-getting. It comes from rather a low instinct. Certainly, as far as my observation goes, it is rarely met in combination with the finer or more interesting traits of character. I have known, and known tolerably well, a good

many "successful" men — "big" financially — men famous
during the last half-century; and a less interesting crowd I
do not care to encounter. Not one that I have ever known
would I care to meet again, either in this world or in the
next; nor is one of them associated in my mind with the
idea of humour, thought or refinement. A set of mere money-
getters and traders, they were essentially unattractive and
uninteresting. The fact is that money-getting, like everything else, calls for a special aptitude and great concentration; and for it I did not have the first to any marked degree, and to it I never gave the last. So, in now summing
up, I may account myself fortunate in having got out of my
ventures as well as I did.

This is by no means the language of a man who, like my acquaintance from the Middle West, is sustained and emboldened
by the consciousness of being in cooperation with his fellows —
far from it. It will be enough, I think, to intimate pretty dearly
the divisive and separatist tendency of education, and to show
the serious risk that a young person of the present day incurs in
acquiring an education. As matters now stand, I believe that he
should not take that risk, and that any one advising or tempting
him to take it is doing him a great disservice.

IV

An educated young man likes to think; he likes ideas for their
own sake and likes to deal with them disinterestedly and objec-
tively. He will find this taste an expensive one, much beyond his
means, because the society around him is thoroughly indisposed
towards anything of the kind. It is preeminently a society, as John
Stuart Mill said, "in which the test of a great mind is agreeing in
the opinions of small minds." In any department of American life
this is indeed the only final test; and this fact is in turn a fair
measure of the extent to which our society is inimical to thought.
The president of Columbia University is reported in the press as
having said the other day that "thinking is one of the most unpopular amusements of the human race. Men hate it largely be-

cause they can not do it. They hate it because if they enter upon it as a vocation or avocation it is likely to interfere with what they are doing." This is an interesting admission for the president of Columbia to make — interesting and striking. Circumstances have enabled our society to get along rather prosperously, though by no means creditably, without thought and without regard for thought, proceeding merely by a series of improvisations; hence it has always instinctively resented thought, as likely to interfere with what it was doing. Therefore, the young person who has cultivated the ability to think and the taste for thinking is at a decided disadvantage, for this resentment is now stronger and more heavily concentrated than it ever was. Any doubt on this point may be easily resolved by an examination of our current literature, especially our journalistic and periodical literature.

The educated lad also likes to cultivate a sense of history. He likes to know how the human mind has worked in the past, and upon this knowledge he instinctively bases his expectations of its present and future workings. This tends automatically to withdraw him from many popular movements and associations because he knows their like of old, and knows to a certainty how they will turn out. In the realm of public affairs, for instance, it shapes his judgment of this-or-that humbugging political nostrum that the crowd is running eagerly to swallow; he can match it all the way back to the politics of Rome and Athens, and knows it for precisely what it is. He can not get into a ferment over this-or-that exposure of the almost incredible degradation of our political, social and cultural character; over an investigation of Tammany's misdoings; over the Federal Government's flagitious employment of the income-tax law to establish a sleeping-partnership in the enterprises of gamblers, gangsters, assassins and racketeers; over the wholesale looting of public property through official connivance; over the crushing burden which an ever-increasing bureaucratic rapacity puts upon production. He knows too much about the origin and nature of government not to know that all these matters are representative, and that nothing significant can be done about them except by a self-sprung change of character in the people represented. He is aware, with Edmund Burke, that "there never was for any long time a corrupt representation of a virtuous people, or a mean, sluggish, careless people that ever had a good government of any form." He perceives, with Ibsen, that "men still call for special revolutions, for revolutions in politics, in externals. But all that sort of thing is trumpery. It is the soul of man that must revolt."

Thus in these important directions, and in others more or less like them, the educated youth starts under disadvantages from which the trained youth is free. The trained youth has no incentive to regard these matters except as one or another of them may bear upon his immediate personal interest. Again, while education does not make a gentleman, it tends to inculcate certain partialities and repugnances which training does not tend to inculcate, and which are often embarrassing and retarding. They set up a sense of self-respect and dignity as an arbiter of conduct, with a jurisdiction far outreaching that of law and morals; and this is most disadvantageous. Formerly this disadvantage was not so pressing, but now it is of grave weight. At the close of Mr. Jefferson's first term, some of his political advisers thought it would be a good move for him to make a little tour in the North and let the people see him. He replied, with what now seems an incomprehensible austerity, that he was "not reconciled to the idea of a chief magistrate parading himself through the several States as an object of public gaze, and in quest of an applause which, to be valuable, should be purely voluntary." In his day a chief magistrate could say that and not lose by it; Mr. Jefferson carried every northern State except Connecticut and every southern State except Maryland. At the present time, as we have lately been reminded, the exigencies of politics have converted candidacy for public office into an exact synonym for an obscene and repulsive exhibitionism.

Again, education tends towards a certain reluctance about push-ing oneself forward; and in a society so notoriously based on the principle of each man for himself, this is a disadvantage. Charles Francis Adams's younger brother Henry, in his remarkable book called *The Education of Henry Adams*, makes some striking obser-vations on this point. Henry Adams was no doubt the most ac-complished man in America, probably the ablest member of the family which as a whole has been the most notable in American public service since 1776. His youth was spent in acquiring an uncommonly large experience of men and affairs. Yet he says that his native land never offered him but one opportunity in the whole course of his life, and that was an assistant-professorship of history at Harvard, at four dollars a day; and he says further that he "could have wept on President Eliot's shoulder in hysterics, so grateful was he for the rare goodwill that inspired the compli-ment." He recalls that at the age of thirty:

> No young man had a larger acquaintance and relation-ship than Henry Adams, yet he knew no one who could help him. He was for sale, in the open market. So were many of his friends. All the world knew it, and knew too that they were cheap; to be bought at the price of a me-chanic. There was no concealment, no delicacy and no illusion about it. Neither he nor his friends complained; but he felt sometimes a little surprised that, as far as he knew, no one seeking in the labour-market even so much as in-quired about their fitness ... The young man was required to impose himself, by the usual business methods, as a ne-cessity on his elders, in order to compel them to buy him as an investment. As Adams felt it, he was in a manner ex-pected to blackmail.

Such were the disabilities imposed upon the educated person fifty years ago, when as Adams says, "the American character showed singular limitations which sometimes drove the student of civilized man to despair." Owing to increased tension of the economic system, they are now much heavier. Even more than then, the educated youth emerges, as Adams and his friends did, to find himself "jostled of a sudden by a crowd of men who seem to him ignorant that there is a thing called ignorance; who have forgotten how to amuse themselves; who can not even understand that they are bored."

One might add a few more items to the foregoing, chiefly in the way of spiritual wear and tear — specific discouragements, irritations, disappointments — which in these days fall to the lot of the educated youth, and which the trained youth escapes; but I have mentioned enough for the purpose. Now, it is quite proper to say that the joys and satisfactions of being educated should be brought out as an offset. One can not get something for nothing, nor can one "have it going and coming." If an education is in itself as rewarding a thing as it is supposed to be, it is worth some sacrifice. It is unreasonable to court the joy of making oneself at home in the world's culture, and at the same time expect to get Standard Oil dividends out of it. Granted that your educated lad is out of step, lonesome, short on business acumen and concentration, and all the rest of it — well, he has his education; nobody can get it away from him; his treasure is of the sort that moth and rust do not corrupt, and stock-market operators can not break through and mark down quotations on it. Agreed that if Charles Francis Adams had not been an educated gentleman he might have become another Gould, Fisk, Harriman, Rockefeller, Huntington, Morgan; but given his choice, would he have swapped off his education and its satisfactions for the chance to change places with any of them? Certainly not.

Certainly not; but times have changed. If economic opportunity were now what it was even in Henry Adams's day, a young person just starting out might think twice about balancing the advantages of an education against its disadvantages. In that day, by a little stretching and with a little luck, a young person might come to some sort of compromise with society, but the chance of

this is now so remote that no one should take it. Since the clos-
ing of the frontier, in or about 1890, economic exploitation has
tightened up at such a rate that compromise is hardly possible. It
takes every jot of a young person's attention and energy merely to
catch on and hang on; and as we have been noticing these last
two years, he does not keep going any too well, even at that. The
question is not one of being willing to make reasonable sacrifices;
it is one of accepting every reasonable prospect of utter destitu-
tion. The joys and satisfactions of an education are all that Commencement orators say they are, and more; yet there is force in
the Irishman's question, "What's the world to a man when his
wife's a widdy?"

V

Things may change for the better, in time; no doubt they will.
Economic opportunity may, by some means unforeseen at present,
be released from the hold of its present close monopoly. The
social value of intellect and character may some day be rediscovered, and the means of their development may be rehabilitated.
Were I to be alive when all this happens, I should take up my
parable of five years ago, and speak as strongly for education as I
did then. But I shall not be alive, and I suspect also that none of
the young persons now going out into the world from our training-schools will be alive; so there is no practical point to considering this prospect at present. Hence I can only raise my voice in
recantation from the mourner's bench, a convert by force of expediency if not precisely in principle — rice-Christian style, perhaps, and yet, what is one to say? I belong to an earlier time, and
for one reason or another the matter of rice does not present
itself as an over-importunate problem, but nevertheless I see that
the Christians have now "cornered" all the rice, so I can not
advise young persons to do as I and my contemporaries did. No,
they are right, their training-schools are right; Richard Roe and I

are wrong. Let them be honest Christians if they can possibly manage the will-to-believe — one can make astonishing successes with that sometimes by hard trying — but if not, let them be rice-Christians, they can do no better.

Gastein, June, 1932
Harper's – September, 1932

But when the Declaration of Independence was drafted Mr. Jefferson wrote "life, liberty, and the pursuit of happiness" . . . his colleagues . . . let the alteration stand . . . It was a revolutionary change.

Life, Liberty, and . . .

For almost a full century before the Revolution of 1776 the classic enumeration of human rights was "life, liberty, and property." The American Whigs took over this formula from the English Whigs, who had constructed it out of the theories of their seventeenth-century political thinkers, notably John Locke. It appears in the Declaration of Rights, which was written by John Dickinson and set forth by the Stamp Act Congress. In drafting the Constitution of Massachusetts in 1779 Samuel and John Adams used the same formula. But when the Declaration of Independence was drafted Mr. Jefferson wrote "life, liberty, and the pursuit of happiness," and although his colleagues on the committee, Franklin, Livingston, Sherman, and Adams, were pretty well tinctured with Whig philosophy, they let the alteration stand.

It was a revolutionary change. "The pursuit of happiness" is of course an inclusive term. It covers property rights, because obviously if a person's property is molested, his pursuit of happiness is interfered with. But there are many interferences which are not aimed at specific property rights; and in so wording the Declaration as to cover all these interferences, Mr. Jefferson immensely broadened the scope of political theory — he broadened the idea of what government is for. The British and American Whigs thought the sociological concern of government stopped with abstract property rights. Mr. Jefferson thought it went further; he thought that government ought to concern itself with the larger and inclusive right to pursue happiness.

II

This clause of the Declaration has been a good deal in my mind lately because for the best part of a year I have been moving about in several countries, and have noticed that hardly anybody in any of them seemed happy. I do not say that the people I saw were sullen or gloomy, or that they no longer occupied themselves in their usual ways. What struck me was, simply, that the general level of happiness was not so high as I had been accustomed to see it some years ago. The people did not act like free people. They seemed under a shadow, enervated, sat upon. They showed little of the spontaneity of spirit which is a sure mark of happiness; even in their amusements they behaved like people who have something on their minds. Moreover, this decline of spirit apparently had little to do with "prosperity" or the lack of it. For all I could see, the prosperous were as dispirited as the unprosperous, and the well-to-do seemed not much, if any, happier than the poor.

But the interesting thing about this moral enervation was that so much of it, practically all of it, was attributable to nothing else but state action. Any thoughtful observer could not help seeing that it arose chiefly out of a long series of positive interferences with the individual's right to pursue happiness. Whether or not these interventions were justifiable on other grounds, it was clear that if the state really had any concern with the individual's pursuit of happiness, it had made a most dreadful mess of its responsibility. I noticed with interest, too, that all the countries I visited had some sort of political structure that could be called republican. That is to say, their sovereignty nominally resided in the people, and the people nominally created their governments. This brought to my mind Paine's saying that "when we suffer or are exposed to the same miseries *by* a government which we might expect in a country *without* government, our calamity is heightened by the reflection that we furnish the means whereby we suffer." As an exercise of the scientific imagination, I tried to make a fair conjecture at the question whether the aggregate of these peoples' happiness was appreciably greater under the governments they had than it would be if they had no government at all. I could not make out that it was. I am not prepared with any elaborate defence of my estimate, but I think I could at least set up a pretty good case for the proposition that they were not nearly so happy as they would be if their governments had been considerably less paternalistic.

I am very far from suggesting that these governments deliberately set out to make their peoples unhappy. The question of motive need not come in at all. In fact, we may admit that by every one of its interventions the state intended to raise the general level of happiness, and actually thought it would do so. The only thing we need observe is that quite evidently it had not done so, and that if it had acted differently it might have succeeded better. By consequence, if it were acting differently now, the prospect for an increase in these peoples' happiness hereafter might be brighter than it is.

How, then, should the state act? What is the utmost that the state can do to raise the general level of happiness? Mr. Jefferson's answer to this question can be put in few words — that it should mind its own business. But what is its business? In Mr. Jefferson's view its business is to protect the individual from the aggressions and trespasses of his neighbors, and beyond this, to leave him strictly alone. The state's whole duty is, first, to abstain entirely from any positive regulation of the individual's conduct; and, second, to make justice easily and costlessly accessible to every applicant. In its relations with the individual, the code of state action should be purely negative, more negative by 20 per cent than the Ten Commandments. Its legitimate concern is with but two matters: first, freedom; second, justice.

III

This was Mr. Jefferson's notion of the state's part in bringing about an ideal social order. All his life was devoted to the doctrine that the state should never venture into the sphere of positive regulation. Its only intervention upon the individual should be the negative one of forbidding the exercise of rights in any way that interferes with the free exercise of the rights of others. According to this idea, one could see that the unhappiness and enervation which I was everywhere observing as due to state action were due to state action entirely outside the state's proper sphere. They were due to the state's not minding its own business but making a series of progressive encroachments on the individual's business. They were due to the state's repeated excursions out of the realm of negative coercion into the realm of positive coercion.

The frequency, variety, and extent of these excursions as disclosed by the last twenty years of European history are almost beyond belief. Tracing them in detail would be impracticable here, and is probably unnecessary. Any one acquainted with European conditions twenty years ago will be pretty well able to judge by how much the margin of existence, which the individual is free to dispose of for himself, has been reduced. Here or there in Europe the state now undertakes to tell the individual what he may buy and sell; it limits his freedom of movement; it tells him what sort of quarters he may occupy; what he may manufacture; what he may eat; what the discipline of his family shall be; what he shall read; what his modes of entertainment shall be. It "manages" his currency, "manages" the worth of his labor, his sales-prices and buying-prices, his credit, his banking facilities, and so on with an almost limitless particularity; and it keeps an enormous, highly articulated bureaucracy standing over him to see that its orders are carried out.

This, too, when one considers only the positive coercions that the state applies directly to the individual. When one considers also those that it applies indirectly, one sees that the individual's margin of free existence has well-nigh disappeared bodily. These coercions take place when the state invades fields of endeavor that were formerly occupied by private enterprise, and either competes with private enterprise or supplants it. In the countries that I visited, the state now appears variously as railway-operator, ship-operator, shipbuilder, house-builder, clothier, shoemaker, gunmaker, wholesale and retail tobacconist, match-seller, banker and money-lender, news-purveyor, radio-broadcaster, market-operator, aviation-enterpriser, letter-carrier, parcel-carrier, telegraphist, telephonist, pawnbroker. The state has also invaded the field of eleemosynary effort, or what is called, I believe, "social service." Thus the state now appears as grand almoner, giving away immense largesse in the form of doles or wage-supplements. It also appears as employer-at-large, improvising work for those who have none. It also appears as educator-in-chief, chief sanitary inspector, chief arbitrator, chief druggist and chemist, chief agriculturist, and in many like rôles; in one country I noticed that the state had even undertaken a loose monopoly of the dissemination of culture! I can think of only one line of human activity — religion — which state meddling has of late years tended rather to decrease than to increase. Formerly the state was a considerable purveyor of religious opportunity, but now it does very little actively in that way, its subsidies being mostly confined to tax-exemption, as in the United States.

IV

By way of consequence, two things are noticeable. The first one is that whatever the state has accomplished outside its own proper field has been done poorly and expensively. This is an old story, and I shall not dwell upon it. No complaint is more common, and none better founded, than the complaint against officialism's inefficiency and extravagance. Every informed person who is at the same time disinterested is aware — often by harassing experience — that as compared with the administration of private enterprise, bureaucratic administration is notoriously and flagrantly slow, costly, inefficient, improvident, unadaptive, unintelligent, and that it tends directly to become corrupt. The reasons why this is so, and must be so, have often been set forth — the classic document in the case is Herbert Spencer's essay called *The New Toryism* — so I shall not go over them afresh, but merely cite one sample comparison which I was able to make, not in Europe, but here in America, and only the other day. I choose it merely for its vividness, since it concerns the one state enterprise which at present is considered the most laudable, most necessary, and most highly humanitarian.

About a week ago, I had by sheer accident an "inside" chance to compare American state enterprise with private enterprise in the matter of relief for certain enormous batches of destitute vagrants. The contrast was most impressive. If the cooperation of private enterprise had not stayed steadily on the spot to read the Riot Act to state enterprise, to show it which way to go and how to start, where to get off and how to stop when it got there, and in a general way hold its hand from beginning to end, those vagrants would have stood the best chance in the world not only of starving but of freezing, for a sudden spell of very bitter weather had just come on.

The clear consenting testimony of all political history certifies this incident as a standard specimen of state efficiency. The post office is often cited as an example of a state commercial monopoly that is well and cheaply administered. It is nothing of the kind. The post office merely sorts mail and distributes it. Private enterprise transports it; and as John Wanamaker said when he was Postmaster General, private enterprise would be only too glad to take over everything that the post office now does, do it much better and for much less money, and make an attractive profit out of it at that.

The second noticeable consequence of the state's activity in everybody's business but its own is that its own business is monstrously neglected. According to our official formula expressed in the Declaration, as I have said, the state's business is, first, with freedom; second, with justice. In the countries I visited, freedom and justice were in a very dilapidated condition; and the striking thing was that the state not only showed complete indifference to their breakdown, but appeared to be doing everything it could to break them down still further. As James Madison wrote in a letter to Mr. Jefferson in 1794, the state was busily "turning every contingency into a resource for accumulating force in the government," with a most callous disregard, not only of freedom and justice, but of common honesty. Every few days brought out some new and arbitrary confiscation of individual rights. Labor was progressively confiscated, capital was progressively confiscated, even speech and opinion were progressively confiscated; and naturally, in the course of this procedure anything like freedom and justice was ignored.

In short, I thought the people might fairly be said to be living for the state. The state's fiscal exactions, necessary to support its incursions into everybody's business but its own, were so great that their payment represented the confiscation of an unconscionable amount of the individual's labor and capital. Its positive regulations and coercions were so many, so inquisitorial, and their points of incidence upon the individual were so various, as to confiscate an unconscionable amount of his time and attention. Its enormously advantaged presence in so many fields of enterprise that are properly free and competitive confiscated an unconscionable share of his initiative and interest. It seemed to me that whichever way the individual turned, the state was promptly on hand to meet him with some form of positive coercion; at every step he was met by a regulation, an exaction, or a menace. Not daily but hourly, in the course of my travels, there occurred to me Mr. Henry L. Mencken's blunt characterization of the state as "the common enemy of all honest, industrious, and decent men."

So indeed it seemed. Putting the case in plain language, the individual was living in a condition of servitude to the state. The fact that he "furnished the means by which he suffered" — that he was a member of a nominally sovereign body — made his condition none the less one of servitude. Slavery is slavery whether it be voluntary or involuntary, nor is its character at all altered by the nature of the agency that exercises it. A man is in slavery when all his rights lie at the arbitrary discretion of some agency other than himself; when his life, liberty, property, and the whole direction of his activities are liable to arbitrary and irresponsible confiscation at any time — and this appeared to be the exact relation that I saw obtaining between the individual and the state.

V

This relation corresponds to a political theory precisely oppo-site to the one set forth in the Declaration. It is not a new theory; it is merely "cauld kail made het again," as the Scots say — it is the old doctrine of absolutism in a new mode or form. The theory behind the Declaration is that the state exists for the good of the individual and that the individual has certain rights which are not derived from the state, but which belong to him in virtue of his humanity. He was born with them, and they are "unalien-able." No power may infringe on them, least of all the state. The language of the Declaration is most explicit on this point. It is *to secure these rights*, Mr. Jefferson wrote, that governments are insti-tuted among men. That is what government is for. The state may not invade these rights or abridge them; all it may do is to protect them, and that is the purpose of its existence.

The new absolutist theory of politics is exactly the opposite of this. The individual exists for the good of the state. He has no natural rights, but only such rights as the state provisionally grants him; the state may suspend them, modify them, or take them away at its own pleasure. Mussolini sums up this doctrine very handsomely in a single phrase, "Everything for the state; nothing outside the state; nothing against the state," and this is only an extension to the logical limit of the doctrine set forth in England by Carlyle, Professor Huxley, Matthew Arnold, and many others in the last century.

This idea, the absolutist idea of the state, seems to be very generally prevalent at the moment. The great majority of social philosophers and publicists treat it as matter-of-course; not only in Europe, where some form of theoretical absolutism has always been more or less in vogue, but also in America, where the idea of government, as expressed officially in the Declaration, runs all the other way. Since my return here I cannot help noticing that the rank and file of Americans seem to be extremely well reconciled to the idea of an absolute state, for the most part on pragmatic or "practical" grounds; that is to say, having found the frying-pan of a misnamed and fraudulent "rugged individualism" too hot for comfort, they are willing to take a chance on the fire. If only one be tactful enough not to name the hated names of Socialism, Bolshevism, Communism, Fascism, Marxism, Hitlerism, or what not, one finds no particular objection to the single essential doctrine that underlies all these systems alike — the doctrine of an absolute state. Let one abstain from the coarse word *slavery* and one discovers that in the view of many Americans — I think probably most of them — an actual slave-status is something that is really not much to be dreaded, but rather perhaps to be welcomed, at least provisionally. Such is the power of words.

The absolutist doctrine seems to assume that the state is a kind of organism, something that has an objective existence apart from the mere aggregation of individuals who make it up. Mussolini speaks of the state much as certain hierophants speak of the Church — as though if all its citizens died off overnight, the state would go on existing as before. So in the last generation Carlyle said that the state should be "the vital articulation of many individuals into a new collective individual"; and one hears the same sort of thing continually from the neo-absolutists of the present day.

No doubt this conception of the state has poetic truth, and to that extent there is a great deal in it. But in its practical relations with the individual, the state acts as though the idea also had scientific truth, which it manifestly has not. Merely reducing the matter to its lowest terms, as I did a moment ago, shows that it has not. Suppose every German died tonight, would the Hitlerian absolute state exist tomorrow in any but a strictly poetic sense? Clearly not.

Again, the absolutist rejection of the idea of natural rights lands one straight in the midst of the logical tangle that so baffled Herbert Spencer. If the individual has no rights but those that the state gives him, and yet if, according to republican theory, sovereignty resides in the people, we see a strange sort of sequence. Here we have a sovereign aggregation of individuals, none of whom has any rights of any kind. They create a government, which creates rights and then confers them on the individuals who created it. The plain man's wits do not hold out through this sequence, nor yet did Spencer's. "Surely," he says, "among metaphysical phantoms the most shadowy is this which supposes a thing to be obtained by creating an agent, which creates the thing, and then confers the thing on its own creator!"

But I do not intend to discuss these doctrines further; least of all do I intend to follow them into the shadowy realms of metaphysics. The thing that I am interested in for the moment is the pursuit of happiness. The question I wish to raise is whether it is possible for human beings to be happy under a regime of absolutism. By happiness I mean happiness. I do not mean the exhilaration arising from a degree of physical well-being, or the exaltation that comes from a brisk run of money-getting or money-spending, or the titillations and distractions brought on by the appeal to raw sensation, or the fanatical quasi-religious fervor that arises from participation in some mass-enterprise — as in Russia and Germany, at the moment. I refer to a stable condition of mind and spirit quite above anything of that kind; a condition so easily recognized and so well understood that I do not need to waste space on trying to define it.

Mr. Pickwick's acquaintance, Mr. Jack Hopkins, the young surgeon, thought a surgical operation was successful if it was skilfully done. Mr. Pickwick, on the other hand, thought it was successful if the patient got well. While in Europe I read a good many essays and speeches about public affairs, and they impressed me as having been written mostly from Mr. Jack Hopkins's point of view. Their burden was that the state's progressive confiscations, exactions and positive coercions, its progressive dragooning of the individual under bureaucratic management, were infallibly going to usher in a new Era of Plenty. If the state only kept on enlarging the scope of officialism, only kept on increasing its encroachments upon the individual's available margin of existence, it would round out an excellent social order and put it on a permanent footing.

Well, possibly. I have no inclination to dispute it, since even if the state were sure to do all this, I still have a previous question to raise. Like Mr. Pickwick, I am interested to know what the individual is going to be like when it is done. Let us make an extreme hypothesis. Let us suppose that instead of being slow, extravagant, inefficient, wasteful, unadaptive, stupid, and at least by tendency corrupt, the state changes its character entirely and becomes infinitely wise, good, disinterested, efficient, so that any one may run to it with any little two-penny problem and have it solved for him at once in the wisest and best way possible. Suppose the state close-herds the individual so far as to forestall every conceivable consequence of his own bad judgment, weakness, incompetence; suppose it confiscates all his energy and resources and employs them much more advantageously all round than he can employ them if left to himself. My question still remains — what sort of person is the individual likely to become under those circumstances?

I raise this question only because no one else seems ever to think of raising it, and it strikes me as worth raising. In all I have heard or read, in public or private, during the last four years, it has never once come up. I do not pretend to answer it. I raise it merely in the hope of starting the idea in the minds of others, for them to think about and answer for themselves, if they think it worth while to do so.

Can any individual be happy when he is continually conscious of not being his own man? Can the pursuit of happiness be satis-factorily carried on when its object is prescribed and its course charted by an agency other than oneself? In short, is happiness compatible with a condition of servitude, whether the voluntary servitude of the "yes-man" or the involuntary servitude of the conscript? How far is happiness conditioned by character, by keep-ing the integrity of one's personality inviolate, by the cultivation of self-respect, dignity, independent judgment, a sense of justice; and how far is all this compatible with membership in a conscript society? This is what I should like to hear discussed, for one hears nothing of it. If we might have this topic thoroughly threshed out for us in public now and again, I for one would not ask for an-other word about "a planned economy" and similar matters for a long time.

Crossing to America after the experiences I have mentioned, I read for the third time Mr. Aldous Huxley's *Brave New World*. Soon after arriving I read the extraordinary production called *Karl and the Twentieth Century*. I cannot recommend these books for purposes of entertainment; they are neither light nor particu-larly cheerful. One thing they do, however, and they do it ex-ceedingly well. They throw a strong light, a very strong light indeed, upon what was probably in Mr. Jefferson's mind when he revised the classic enumeration of man's natural rights, and made it read, "life, liberty, and the pursuit of happiness." What I have seen since I landed has made me think it is high time for Ameri-cans to wake up to what the state is doing, and ask themselves a few plain questions about it. There are plenty of examples to show what a conscript society is like — well, do they want to live in one? There are plenty of examples to show what sort of people a conscript society breeds — is that the sort of people they want to be? Do they like the idea of a slave-status with a coercive and militant state as their owner? If they do, I should say they are getting what they want about as fast as is reasonably possible; and if they do not, my impression is that they had better not lose much time about being heard from.

Scribner's – March, 1935

Mr. Jefferson remarked that "it is the manners and spirit of a people which preserve a republic in vigor. A degeneracy in these is a canker which soon eats to the heart of its laws and constitution."

A Study in Manners

American history has been of late so largely rediscovered and rewritten that one would hardly imagine there were many left to share the late Mr. Harding's amiable illusions about the Founding Fathers. Yet there must be some, for in the campaign of 1924 I was present when one of the candidates got a rousing hand of applause for telling his audience that the Fathers had established a government of the people, for the people, and by the people! I was greatly tempted to ask him whether he had ever heard of a publication called the *Federalist*, and if not, whether he would like to borrow my old calf-bound copy and browse around in it a little here and there, before committing himself further to this preposterous proposition.

The Founding Fathers, in fact, did no such thing — far from it. They had the greatest horror of popular government; they dreaded it like the plague. A view of the Constitutional Convention of 1787 as a disinterested and high-minded rivalry between two abstract political theories is very pretty, but sheer fiction. The Fathers were not theorists. There was no discount on their ability; in that respect they were one of the most extraordinary and remarkable groups that the world ever saw; but their disinterestedness was not, perhaps, quite what romantic tradition of the school-books cracks it up to be. As Mr. Dooley remarked, they "were mostly in the fish-ile business," and the Constitutional Convention was made up of hard-headed and wary brethren who were not strong on abstractions but were very clear about what they wanted and uncommonly skilful in framing the right kind of air-tight charter for getting it. Their enthusiasm for popular government was about as strong as the late Judge Gary's or Mr. Pierpont Morgan's, and had the same motive. As a matter of fact, government is at this moment much nearer the hands of the people than the Founding Fathers left it, or than they ever intended it should be.

A coarse and indiscriminate glorification of the Fathers does great disservice to their memory because, among other reasons, it tends to obscure the really good and fine things which they occasionally did. The school-book's picture of them is like a Gothic fresco; everything is flat, without any perspective or relief. If all the Fathers were uniformly noble, public-spirited, and disinterested all the time, then all their acts were equipollent and none more impressive than another. When the average of nobility and disinterestedness is one hundred per cent twenty-four hours a day, even a Founding Father cannot go over it. If, however, revaluation brings the average down somewhere near erring humanity's normal figure, the occasional hundred per cent achievement stands out in proper perspective and can be appraised accordingly. In the course of a casual occupation with the doings of the Fathers, I lately happened on one of these achievements which moved me profoundly; and yet the act itself did not, I think, stir my imagination as much as did the reason that the Father gave for doing it.

In the year 1800, the year of the great final contest between the Federalists and the Republicans, the outgoing legislature of New York was Federalist and the newly-elected legislature was anti-Federalist. Since the stripe of the presidential electors was at that time determined by that of the legislature, this boded great danger to the Federalist national ticket; it threatened to seat Mr. Jefferson in the presidential chair; and this prospect so frightened Alexander Hamilton that he addressed a letter to the Governor of New York, who was John Jay, urging him to recall the adjourned legislature, for the purpose of enacting a measure to defeat the will of the people and save the national election for the party.

This letter was a model of strength and speciousness. Hamilton assured Governor Jay that "in times like these in which we live, it will not do to be over-scrupulous," and that "the scruples of delicacy and propriety, as relative to a common course of things, ought to yield to the extraordinary nature of the crisis. They ought not to hinder the taking of a legal and constitutional step to prevent an athiest religion and a fanatic in politics from getting possession of the helm of state." Hamilton knew his man, and he laid all the stress he could upon the one point that he knew would most of all stick in the Governor's craw; but to no purpose. Governor Jay did not move in the matter. There is no record, as far as I know, that he even acknowledged Hamilton's letter. After his death, nearly thirty years later, it was found among his papers, inscribed, "Proposing a measure for party purposes, which I do not think it would be becoming to adopt."

Governor Jay had unusual ability and the most nearly flawless character, probably, of any man in the public life of that time. Mr. Beveridge, in his biography of Marshall, characterizes him sympathetically as "the learned an gentle Jay." In principle he was as strong a Federalist as Hamilton himself, for by all the force of birth, education, and circumstances he was an aristocrat. Quite conscientiously, he was one of those whom Mr. Jefferson described under a striking figure, as believing that some of mankind were born with saddles on the backs, and others born booted and spurred to ride them. While not a purblind Anglophile, he had as long as possible favored a mild and conciliatory policy toward England in the pre-Revolutionary period, and in 1794 he had been burned in effigy all over the country for the execution of the treaty which bears his name. He had a deep distrust of popular government, and viewed the prospective triumph of Mr. Jefferson, the "fanatic in politics," with apprehension and distaste. After Mr. Jefferson's election, indeed, he refused further preferment, turned his back upon public life, and though at the height of his powers, passed the rest of his days in retirement.

Why may not a wayward scion of his stock say of him what any radical-minded outsider would surely say, that he was a benighted old Tory? He could quite legally and constitutionally have made the move that Hamilton implored him to make, for the old legislature still had tenure of office for seven or eight weeks. If he had done so, no doubt, public sentiment in New York State would have run pretty high; but that need not have concerned him, for, with his own party continued in power at Washington, the Administration would have taken royal good care of him and given him his pick of patronage. Every predilection of his own was in favour of Hamilton's suggestion. A devout man, he might well have let the end justify the means of keeping a person of Mr. Jefferson's well-known unorthodoxy out of the Presidency. Yet he looked at the opportunity and passed it by in silence because *he did not think it would be becoming* to embrace it.

II

One rubs one's eyes in astonishment. What an extraordinary reason to assign for a decision of such profound political significance! What an extraordinary standard by which to appraise political conduct! That an act is illegal might conceivably give some shadow of reason why a politician should object to it. The exceptional politician might even, indeed, in an atrabilious moment, object to an act because he found it immoral or dishonest. Objection, however, to an act which is neither illegal nor dishonest, merely because it is *unbecoming* — this represents a distinction which, to put it gently, few politicians of today could be expected to draw under any circumstances, let alone such circumstances as pressed so powerfully upon Governor Jay.

Let us suppose a case that would stand in some kind of rough correspondence. Governor Smith is said to be one of the most honest and disinterested men in our public life, and Senator La Follette occupied, in the campaign of 1924, a position which in one or two essential respects resembled that of Mr. Jefferson's in 1800. Suppose now that Senator La Follette's election, as far as one could see, had hung on the question whether Governor Smith would or would not turn a political trick that was legal and regular enough, but *unbecoming* — well, without the least wish to disparage Governor Smith, whom I do not know and never saw, and whose public acts as a rule impress me favourably, I merely ask what, in such a case, might one expect? In the campaign of 1924, Senator La Follette was almost as much dreaded, execrated and maligned as was Mr. Jefferson in the campaign of 1800. Would Governor Smith consent to see his own party lose a national election, and the Cagliostro of politics take the Presidency, rather than do something that had no more against it than mere shabbiness and indecency?

One might make use of Governor Jay's fine action, I suppose, to show how disreputably low the personnel of our public service has fallen in these degenerate days, and how hard we should all work to get good men in office and to keep them there. Yet for one reason or another, I have somewhat of the Psalmist's diffidence about meddling with these "great matters which are too high for me," preferring to turn all that kind of thing over to the Liberal publicists. *Beati pauperes spiritu!* — I bring this incident forward only because I myself greatly enjoy dwelling on it; and I enjoy dwelling on it because it intimates so clearly the enormous power that resides in a proper sense of what is *becoming*, and the intense satisfaction that one gets out of cultivating and indulging this sense. The incident, in short, provides an excellent study in manners, with which the austere Liberal publicist, absorbed in his great task of educating other people, would probably be impatient, and disdain it as mere shillyshallying, but which is nevertheless not without profit to those humbler spirits, like myself, who are still trying to educate themselves.

The word *manners*, unfortunately, has come to be understood as a synonym for deportment; it includes deportment of course, but it reaches much further. Properly speaking, it covers the entire range of conduct outside the regions where law and morals have control. Goethe, with extraordinary penetration, called attention to certain "conquests which culture has made over nature," and to the importance of observing and maintaining them. Law and morals take cognizance, though very imperfectly and often improperly, of some of these culture-conquests; the rest are in the purview of manners.

In speaking of these culture-conquests as having been won from nature, Goethe's choice of terms is striking and serviceable, but not exact. One would prefer to say, perhaps, that they are conquests which culture has made over the primitive, rather than over nature; for what culture has actually done is to modify certain primitive rights, or cause them to be superseded, through the gradual disclosure of other rights which may be regarded as even more nearly natural, since they comport better with the disposition developed in man as he becomes progressively humanized in society. Culture so exhibits the appropriateness of loyalty to these rights as to inculcate upon us a devotion to them and lead us to acknowledge their validity.

The primitive doctrine of property, for example, now survives in an unmodified form hardly anywhere outside the jungle and the Foreign Offices of imperialist nations. St. Paul, portraying under his admirable figure of the "two selves," the bitter contest that goes on in the individual between the lower and apparent self, governed by what he so finely calls "the suggestions of the flesh and of the current thoughts,"[1] the extemporized, capricious and unconsidered promptings of primitive desire, and the higher and real self, governed by loyalties to which all such impulses are wholly repugnant — here St. Paul, I say, is far more accurate and explicit in his account of the operations of culture than Goethe.

---

[1] θεληματα τηδ σαρκοδ και τῶν ολανοιῶν — Eph. II:3

Yet the great critic's meaning is clear enough. In stealing an inventor's purse, let us say, one must reckon with the law; in stealing his idea, one must reckon with the sense of morals, with the common conscience of mankind; in buying up and suppressing his idea or in exploiting it without adequate compensation, one must reckon with the sense of manners, with the fine and high perceptions established by culture, to which such transactions at once appear mean and low. When Baron Tauchnitz paid full royalties to foreign authors whose works he republished before the days of international copyright, he was governed by a sense of manners; for no law compelled him to pay anything, and the morals of trade would have been quite satisfied if he had paid whatever he chose to pay.

Governor Jay's attitude towards Hamilton's suggestion may be called not only a study in manners, but, with certain explanations carefully made and certain discriminations fully understood, it may justly be called a study in Tory manners. This does not by any manner of means intimate that all Tories have a keen sense of manners, or that the Tory spirit has any natural monopoly of manners, to the exclusion of the radical and liberal spirit. On the contrary, English history exhibits one of the very finest examples of manners in the person of one who was an aristocrat, indeed, but withal, for his time, a great radical — a kind of British Jefferson. By some master-stroke of unconscious irony, the statue of Falkland stands today in a drooping attitude, an attitude of almost despairing despondency — and no wonder! — at the inner entrance to the Houses of Parliament! Lucius Cary, Viscount Falkland, was Secretary of State for a year during the difficult and troubled period just preceding the Civil War. Those who do not know his melancholy and fascinating history do not know the best that England can do in the way of dignifying and ennobling herself in the men she produces. Throughout his tenure of office, Falkland refused either to employ spies or to open letters! Horace Walpole speaks of this as "evincing debility of mind," quite as plausibly as

Hamilton admonished Governor Jay that "in times like these in which we live, it will not do to be over-scrupulous."

But though manners be not a Tory peculium, it is indisputable that a high sense of manners, a fine and delicate perception in matters of conduct, and the supporting strength of character that gives practical effect to both, have been most highly developed and most powerfully propagated by an aristocracy; and an aristocracy is always almost solidly Tory. Where one finds, as in Falkland, or Mr. Jefferson, radical principles and ideals combined with Tory manners, there, of course, one sees about the best that human nature is capable of producing; but such characters are all too seldom met with. I hasten to add that there is no natural reason why the qualities that I have mentioned should not be developed as highly in a democracy, if and when democracy ever comes to pass,[2] I believe they will be much more highly developed; but the fact is that they have been chiefly developed in our modern civilisation through an aristocracy. Indeed, since about all the good one can say of an aristocracy is that it has done this, and since aristocracy is at a pretty heavy discount just now, we can probably afford generosity enough to remember with gratitude that it was no trifling service.

---

[2] I wish to complain against the common and culpable use of the term democracy as a synonym for republicanism. Time and again one hears persons who should know better, talk about democracy in this country, for example, as if something like it really existed here. They discuss "democracy on trial," "democracy's weakness," and so on, when it is perfectly clear that they refer only to the political system known properly as republicanism. The fact is that republicanism, which is a system theoretically based on the right of individual self-expression in politics, has as yet done but little for democracy, and that democracy is less developed in some republican countries, as France and the United States, than in some others, like Denmark, whose political system is nominally non-republican.

It is interesting to remark that a sense of manners, delicacy of perception in matters of conduct, and the strength of character which regularly and resolutely enforces upon oneself their findings, seem to attain their best development in the absence or abeyance of law. Our Indian hunting tribes, for example, never formed a State, and lived without law or government; and there is no end of testimony to the extraordinary and impressive development of manners and the sense of manners, that prevailed among them. Among those peoples which for one reason or another we choose to call civilised, we see a somewhat similar development in a hereditary governing class which can manage the law pretty much to suit itself and hence exists largely above the law. The aristocratic system was in general an incompetent one and its breakdown was inevitable; yet there is some good in the worst of systems, and the good of the aristocratic system was in the stimulation it gave to the sense of manners as a kind of law in itself, outside the purview of either statutory law or morals. It is chiefly to the extra-legal tradition which his hereditary governing class worked out for itself and followed with some degree of faithfulness, that the ordinary Englishman today owes his instinctive power of appraisal, such as it is, in the category of things which he vaguely yet stoutly assures you "aren't done," or which he briefly characterises as "dam' low." Under republicanism this advantage disappears, and the sense of manners, no longer cultivable by this indirect and somewhat adventitious means, must, if cultivated at all, be cultivated more directly and purposefully. Now, there is no doubt, I think, that the sum total of our educational processes does not tend that way. One may be subjected to the resultant influence of our schools, newspapers, pulpits, colleges, average family life, average social life, without gaining any very clear conception of the sense of manners as a kind of law in itself, and indeed without having one's intellectual curiosity much stirred by any consideration of manners, one way or the other.

Half a century ago Ernest Renan acutely pointed out that countries like the United States, which tolerate such imperfections in their educational processes, "would long have to expiate their fault by their intellectual mediocrity, *the vulgarity of their manners*, their superficial spirit, their failure in general intelligence." It would seem that his forecast was substantially accurate; there is testimony to it not only in a rather widespread general restlessness and disatisfaction with the quality of life lived in the United States, but also in innumerable specific complaints that drive us to adopt various forms of censorship and legal regulation. It is also worthy of remark, perhaps, that in our common speech we have constructed a considerable glossary of terms like "getting by," "putting it across," and "putting something over," which intimate the extremely narrow jurisdiction that we habitually assign to manners, and the correspondingly attenuated authority that we attach to the sense of manners.

It may be a form of good one hundred per cent Americanism, I suppose, to declare stoutly that in so enlightened and progressive a civilisation as ours, any abstract consideration of manners is impracticable and superfluous, and that we should deal pragmatically with our standard of manners by progressive improvisation as we go along. While visiting an exhibition of paintings with a friend the other day, I raised some questions of taste and style, and my friend said with a strong air of finality, "But what is taste? Simply your taste, my taste, anybody's taste." In the view of this naïve cynicism, obviously, a general duty to taste is fully discharged when each crude person cleaves happily to what he likes, without troubling himself to ask whether he ought to like it; in other words, without admitting the operation of an artistic conscience, or bethinking himself that the best reason and spirit of the race may have something to say in the premises, and that what it says may conceivably be worth attention. Similarly, too, it may be thought that a general duty to manners is fully discharged when each crude person follows the motions of the herd, or so much of them as his lower and apparent self may elect to follow, and regards his obligations as no more rational or binding, at best, than those of mere fashion.

Yet a cautious old pedant like myself finds it hard to swallow this, because general human experience seems to be against it. Try as he may, he cannot get quite away from the notion that matters like these are not finally to be settled in this happy-go-lucky way, by the whim of each raw person's ordinary self, but by what Aristotle calls "the determination of the judicious" — the judicious being those who have disciplined themselves to take the largest view of general human experience and who have become most sensitive to its testimony. There is a fundamental self-preserving instinct in humanity, which in the end comes out for what is truly lovely, truly elevated and becoming, and will not be permanently satisfied without it. Even that strange son of Balaam, the *homme sensuel moyen*, from Horace down to Mr. Otto H. Kahn, gives this instinct his blessing if not his obedience. It is precisely this instinct which our sturdy Americanism, with its blind insistence on the sanction of law and morals for the exclusive control of conduct, and its equally blind disregard of manners, and of the sense of manners as a law in itself, fails to take into account; and the consequence is that our republican civilisation has an obvious and disconcerting element of instability which it need not and should not have. With aristocracy gone, and republicanism thrown wholly on its own resources in matters of this kind, one would say that it behooves a republic to become aware of the edifying and salutary power resident in a well-developed sense of manners, and to take steps towards concentrating this power and making it effective; and the very first of these steps, logically, is for all of us who have somewhat to do with general education — teachers, editors, preachers, critics, essayists, dramatists, novelists, lecturers — firmly to dissociate from law and morals all courses of conduct that do not belong there, and as firmly to associate them in the category of manners.

III

This, I say, is logical; for what is the use of forever trying mechanically to apply sanctions which are by nature inapplicable and which anyone can see are simply grotesque in the inapplicability, while neglecting others which can be applied intelligently and appropriately? To make a thing illegal, or to put it down as immoral, by sheer fiat, in the face of an instinct which declares it properly to be neither, doe not get one very far in the discouragement of its practice. Cardinal Hayes and Dr. John Roach Straton, for instance, have lately been complaining about the "morals of the young," as exhibited in their amusements, habits of conversation, irregular sex relations, the literature they choose to read and the plays they choose to see. Instinct testifies that in all this these gentlemen have no ground of complaint whatever against morals, and are talking blank nonsense; but that they have an impregnable ground of complaint against manners. If therefore they shifted their ground, they might hope to make an impression which they will never make from where they stand, for they would then have the natural truth of things working with them instead of against them.

When Mr. Taft came out of the White House, he refused to practice his profession and, though a poor man, turned his back upon the emoluments that would have come to him through his prestige as an ex-President. His successor, Mr. Wilson, did the opposite. It is absurd to say that Mr. Taft here showed himself more moral than Mr. Wilson, for morals have no jurisdiction in the premises. Again, when Mr. Jefferson became President, he made it a rule never to take a present from anyone under any circumstances. Other Presidents have not felt it incumbent upon them to do this; but it is utter nonsense to disparage them, or to praise Mr. Jefferson, on the score of morality. Mr. Taft and Mr. Jefferson simply gave an example of admirable manners, of a high and fine perception in matters of conduct, combined with the strength of character to enforce its findings upon themselves at whatever sacrifice; and the others did not.

A symposium dealing with the subject of sexual insurrection has been lately published under the title, "Our Changing Morality." Its original serial title, I believe, was "New Morals for Old." It rather reminded me of Bishop Pontoppidan's chapter on owls in Iceland, for from end to end of the symposium I could find nothing that had any natural connexion with morals, new or old, changing or fixed. Instinct testifies that there is absolutely nothing in the relations of either man or woman with any paramour or syndicate of paramours, which comes properly under the contemplation of morals; and hence any attempt to place the there is nugatory. These matters come properly under the scrutiny, much more effective because wholly appropriate, much more searching because wholly self-imposed, of high-mindedness, delicacy of feeling and perception — in a word, of manners.

Once we give up the pestilent assumption that the only effective sanctions of conduct are those of law and morals, and begin to delimit clearly the field of manners, we shall be by way of discovering how powerful and how easily communicable the sense of manners is, and how efficiently it operates in the very regions where law and morals have so notoriously proven themselves inert. The authority of law and morals does relatively little to build up personal dignity, responsibility and self-respect, while the authority of manners does much. The sacrifices and renunciations exacted by the one authority differ in quality from those exacted by the other, and one assents to them in a different spirit. In a habitual and sensitive regard to the demands of manners, one "lives from a greater depth of being." All this is matter of experience; anyone can try it for himself and find out that it is so. The trouble is that an enormously exaggerated stress on law and morals gives little encouragement to make the trial. It is easier, in a society like ours, to do as the rest do, and mechanically refer all conduct to the sanction of law and morals without troubling oneself to question its applicability or to cast about for a more appropriate authority.

This, in fact, is what our society appears to be doing. It seems competent, therefore, for even the humblest republican intellect to suggest that we may be incurring pretty serious damage through sheer unintelligent indisposition to call things by their right names and take hold of them by the right handles; and that if we stopped our heavy overdoing of law and morals long enough to give consideration to manners, and to the sense of manners as an arbiter of conduct, we might considerably better our prospects. Mr. Jefferson — if I may once more cite that poor old devotee of so many decrepit superstitions — Mr. Jefferson remarked that "it is the *manners* and spirit of a people which preserve a republic in vigor. A degeneracy in these is a canker which soon eats to the heart of its laws and constitution." I also venture to emphasise for special notice by the Americanisers and hundred-per-centers among us, the observation of Edmund Burke that "there ought to be a system of *manners* in every nation which a well-formed mind would be disposed to relish. For us to love our country, our country ought to be lovely."

American Mercury – May, 1925

Perhaps one reason for the falling-off of belief in a continuance of conscious existence is to be found in the quality of life that most of us lead. There is not much in it with which, in any kind of reason, one can associate the idea of immortality.

EARNING IMMORTALITY

The death of Sir A. Conan Doyle has revived a little fitful newspaper comment on spiritism, but hardly as much or of such a quality as might be expected. I think belief in the persistence of human personality after death is not as general as it used to be. The position of modern science, as far as an ignorant man of letters can understand it, seems not a step in advance of that held by Huxley and Romanes in the last century. When Moleschott and Büchner declared there was nothing in the world but matter and force, Huxley said that there was pretty plainly a third thing, i. e., consciousness, which was neither matter nor force or any conceivable modification of either. Its phenomena occurred, as far as we knew them, invariably in association with matter and force, but if any one said they were inseparable from such association, he must ask him how he knew that; and if any said they were not inseparable from it, he must ask the same question. Romanes also observed that the transition from the physics of the brain to the facts of consciousness is unthinkable; and that being so, obviously nothing can be predicated about the persistence of consciousness, even upon the ground of probability, quite as Huxley said. I am unable to see that more modern science has carried us beyond this position of pure agnosticism.

Perhaps one reason for the falling-off of belief in a continuance of conscious existence is to be found in the quality of life that most of us lead. There is not much in it with which, in any kind of reason, one can associate the idea of immortality. Selling bonds, for instance, or promoting finance-companies, seems not to assort with the idea of an existence which can not be imagined to take any account of money or credits. Certain other of our present activities might be imagined as going on indefinitely, such as poetry, music, pure mathematics or philosophy. One can easily imagine an immortal Homer or Beethoven; one can not possibly imagine an immortal Henry Ford or John D. Rockefeller. Probably belief can not transcend experience. If we believe that death is the end of us, very likely it is because we have never had any experience of a kind of life that in any sort of common sense we could think was worth being immortal and we know we have had no such experience. As far as spiritual activity is concerned, most of us who represent this present age are so dead while we live that it seems the most natural thing in the world to assume that we shall stay dead when we die.

I have often wondered whether this idea was not behind the curious interruption that St. Paul makes in his letter to the Corinthian Christians who were disbelievers like ourselves. He gives them all the arguments he can think of, but interrupts himself by throwing in a quotation from the dramatist Menander, which at first sight seems out of place: "Be not deceived; evil communications corrupt a right line of morals." Corinth had a civilization somewhat akin to ours in its ideals; it was highly materialistic, spiritual activity was at a very low level, and appreciation of the things of the spirit was correspondingly weak. St. Paul may have thought, as was no doubt the case, that his converts were unable to believe in a future life, not from any lack of knowledge, but on account of their evil communications — they had never engaged in any kind of activity that was worth being immortal. If they wanted to believe, argument would not help them much; they had better hustle around and get some experience of a different kind of life, and belief would probably follow upon experience, as it usually does. The weakness of spiritism always seemed to me to lie in its neglect of the evidential value of this kind of experience. I know I could witness the most striking spiritist demonstration that I ever heard of, without being moved either to belief or disbelief; but I do not think I could engage long in any purely spiritual activity without being somewhat prepossessed towards belief.

In speculating on such matters, one does not see why life beyond death should not be as much of an achievement as life before death. We all know that life has to be the subject of pretty close management; if we do not adjust ourselves to our physical environment, our physical bodies die pretty promptly; and it is conceivable that a failure to adjust ourselves to our spiritual environment might result similarly. Organized Christianity has always represented immortality as a sort of common heritage; but I never could see why spiritual life should not be conditioned on the same terms as all life, *i. e.*, correspondence with environment. Assuming that man has a distinct spiritual nature, a soul, why should it be thought unnatural that under appropriate conditions of maladjustment, his soul might die before his body does; or that his soul might die without his knowing it? There seems to be a pretty good analogy of nature behind the idea that spiritual existence, if at all possible, is possible only as something to be achieved by purposeful effort. Perhaps relatively very few human personalities will survive physical death — granting that any do — and the great majority simply dissapears. Perhaps this survival awaits him alone who has made it rather strictly his business to discern his spiritual environment and bring himself into adjustment to it; perhaps it is only he who at death, with

all his battles won,
Mounts, *and that hardly*, to eternal life.

Freeman – August, 1930

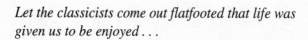

Let the classicists come out flatfooted that life was given us to be enjoyed . . .

THE CLASSICIST'S OPPORTUNITY

The approach of spring attracts attention to the annual spawning of the colleges and universities; and this suggests in turn that the present would be an uncommonly good time for the friends of "the grand old fortifying classical curriculum," the advocates of Greek and Latin studies, to put on their war-paint and return to battle. They have suffered many defeats in recent years; the vocationalists and professors of natural science have had their own way with them for a generation, without let or hindrance. The reason is, in our opinion, that they have been content to remain on the defensive and have let the enemy choose the battle-ground. This is bad strategy. When the vocationalists have challenged the bread-and-butter value of training in the classics, the classicists (we use these terms in a general way, merely to save words) have always gone over to their ground and undertaken to show how much better electrician, chemist, horse-doctor, or what not, a man would become by having studied Greek and Latin literature. In point of fact, they are no doubt right; but it is bad tactics, unimaginative tactics, to rely for ever on sheer defence. The programme of events has now so played into their hand, the stars in their courses have so strikingly arrayed themselves on their side, that we think they ought to hearten up tremendously, and carry the war over into the enemy's country, horse, foot and dragoons.

If we were planning the campaign, we would start it off with a violent frontal assault on the enemy's whole theory of life. If the vocationalist's theory, Murdstone's theory, be the true one; if the world be merely a place to work in, not a place, as Murdstone said, "to be moping and droning in," then it is to the point to discuss the value of the classics in relation to the individual's place in such a world. But now let our friends stand up to the vocationalist and make him defend his theory, make him show cause for holding that the world is such a place. Let them boldly say that the world is nothing of the kind, that it is a place to have fun in, and that you can have ten times more fun and better fun throughout your life if you know Greek and Latin literature, and the more intimately you know it and the closer you stick to it, the more fun you will have. Our friends will remind us that a good deal has been said and written in this vein. Yes, but always on the tacit assumption that the pleasure one has out of life is a sort of by-product, a secondary affair and something to be enjoyed "on the side," as one might say, instead of being life's primary object. Hence there is a general flavour of diffidence and deprecation about all this literature that impairs its apologetic value. Let the classicists come out flatfooted that life was given us to be enjoyed; let them not be afraid of exaggeration or overemphasis; let them resolutely close their ears to any other proposition; and then let them remorselessly take advantage of the support which human nature instinctively gives to that theory of life, and split the ranks of the vocationalists wide open.

There is no time like the present for doing this. The vocationalists have had a clear field; they have ridden organized education like the Old Man of the Sea for twenty-five years, thus bringing out one full generation of adult men and women, in whose hands the affairs of the world now are. They have made an immense success, and no one ought to begrudge them a jot of credit for it. The mechanical organization of society is a marvellous thing, and the development of mechanical facilities for its service is even more marvellous and startling. The only trouble is that nobody seems to be having a very good time. The poor and the exploited are not having a good time, which is to be expected; but the rich and privileged are not having a good time either. All the physical apparatus of happiness is about us, and yet no one, apparently, is having a cent's worth of fun out of it. Well, here is the classicist's opportunity. He can throw his experienced eye, trained by his incessant commerce with the ages, over this anomaly and show cause for it. He can survey the life of our well-to-do and poor alike, and show that about the only fun to be had out of such a life is the search for fun, and show why the desire remains ungratified. He can show by practical example — by horrible example — where, in the preparation for life, certain essential values which have been disregarded by the vocationalist, come in. Thus he has now an advantage which he never had before, in the opportunity to appraise a whole society which represents quite fairly the finished work of his opponents. But we are convinced that he will once more merely fumble this advantage unless he stands immovable upon the bed-rock thesis that life is given to human beings for their enjoyment, that all its other purposes, if it have any, are incidental and ancillary to this one; that the human world by its original intention is not Murdstone's world, not a world of industry and efficiency, but a world of joy.

Freeman – March, 1921

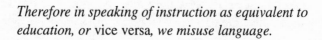

Therefore in speaking of instruction as equivalent to education, or vice versa, *we misuse language.*

TOWARDS A NEW QUALITY-PRODUCT

There are conventions, as well as tricks, in all trades. Every department of social activity being governed chiefly by convention, it is not surprising that the most powerful and far-reaching conventions are the least talked about. We know them, and obey them, but do not speak of them. In Gascony, probably, people do not talk much about gasconades, nor did the city of Gath have much to say about Philistinism. Thus the fundamental conventions that govern our American educational system are never discussed. Criticism and discussion are as a rule confined to matters of method; some of the superficial conventions are sometimes brought under fire; but the fundamental conventions are always left alone.

I propose to bring forward one or two of these conventions and discuss them, by way of preliminary to a practical suggestion. The first convention is that by which we tacitly assume that education and instruction are the same thing, whereas they are really quite different. This is exactly comparable to the convention whereby we assume that republicanism, which is a political system under which everybody has a vote, is the same thing as democracy, which is primarily an economic status, and only secondarily political. Those who speak of the United States as a democracy, for instance, are misusing language most ludicrously, for it is no such thing, never was, and was never intended to be. The Fathers of the Republic were well aware of the difference between a republic and a democracy, and it is no credit to the intelligence of their descendents that the two are now almost invariably confused.

An instructional institution is not at all necessarily educational; whether it be actually so or not depends upon a variety of circumstances which are not usually reckoned with either in the professional or in the popular scale of speech. An instructed pupil is by no means necessarily an educated pupil, not even *in limine*; he is merely a person who has been exposed to instruction, with nothing implied about the effect of the exposure, which even from an instructional, let alone an educational, viewpoint, may quite well be no more than the effect of exposing a duck's back to rain. Whatever education accrues to him depends upon collateral circumstances and conditions. Therefore in speaking of instruction as equivalent to education, or *vice versa*, we misuse language. To avoid pedantry I shall keep on misusing it, for the purposes of this essay, except where the misuse would be ambiguous and perhaps misleading.

In earlier days this distinction was clearer. Ernest Renan long ago drew it with a firm hand, when he spoke of the United States as having set up "a considerable popular instruction without any serious higher education" — probably the most complete and competent criticism of our system that has ever been made, for all other general criticisms that I know of, and most of the special criticisms as well, are finally reducible to it. In the bad old times of the three R's and the deestrick school, the verb *to learn* had a transitive use, and in that use it was quite regularly pronounced *l'arn*. I am old enough to remember this, and hence old enough to mark the disappearance of the transitive form to *l'arn*, in favour of the active verb *to teach*. There seems to be a coincidence here, and a rather interesting one, because, as everyone knows who has tried it, you cannot teach a person anything — unless perchance he knows it it already — but you can l'arn him something. L'arnin' did not in those days, moreover, mean learning, as understood by us of the enlightened present; it did not mean the rather equivocal windfalls that drop in your path of passage from grade to grade of a course of instruction. Not even in its compound *book-l'arnin'* did it mean precisely that. It meant something that somebody had l'arned you. I am not praising those old times, nor do I wish them back; I merely remark that a retrospect upon them discerns traces of this particular, and by no means useless or fantastic, discrimination.

A second fundamental convention that is never discussed is the one by which we assume that everybody ought to go to school. Some hardy educators lately have skirted the fringes of this convention by expressing doubt that everybody ought to go to college. The president of Brown University, in a recent interview, was quite outspoken about this. But as far as I know, no one has questioned the convention that regards all children as proper grist for the mill of the secondary schools. Our "compulsory education laws" as they are fancifully styled, embody this convention; so to question it would probably carry the implication of sedition as well as of heresy. Yet the "school age" which these laws specify counts for nothing, except conventionally; what really counts is school-ability; and the assumption that all children of school age have school-ability is flagrantly at variance with fact. If the law can do anything to encourage children of school-ability, irrespective of age, to go to school; if it can do anything to clear, illuminate, and beautify their path to school and through school, well and good. But the purely conventional content of these laws, in their present form, renders their practical application incompetent, fatuous, and vicious, and they ought to be remodeled in accordance with obvious fact and common sense. There was no need of the army tests to inform us that twelve million — or was it twenty? — of our younger people have not enough force of intellect to get them through the high school. Anyone casually considering a random assortment of our youngsters would be sure there are easily that many who are incapable of getting through any kind of secondary school with any profit whatever to themselves, to anyone else, or to the average of American citizenship.

All this seems extremely odd in view of our reputation for being a practical people. Education in the United States comes to a stupendous amount of money. Aside from public funds, the annual fees and disbursements to private secondary schools, colleges, universities, technical schools, are enormous. Having no statistics, I do not know how the gross sum compares with our annual outlay for chewing-gum, cosmetics, cigarettes, motor-cars, or contraband liquor; but one would be safe in saying that it is large enough to justify some sort of assurance about the kind of product that is being got for it. Yet just this is what no one seems able to give. No one seems to have even any very definite idea of the kind of product that is wanted, or any clear specifications for the kind that our system is attempting to produce.

II

It is probably the convergence of these two fundamental conventions upon the practical conduct of education that causes this uncertainty. Such uncertainty would at all events be the natural consequence of this convergence. Mr. Henry Ford is in no uncertainty about the kind of thing he wishes and intends to produce, or about the public demand for it; and he can give you a clear idea of the distinguishing points and qualities that his product will show when it comes out. This parallel cannot, of course, be pressed too far, because Mr. Ford is dealing with inanimate material, and our educational system is not. It may be usefully employed, however, to show the essential differences established by pure convention between production in Mr. Ford's case and in the case of our educational system.

Suppose there were a convention among the purchasing public which made them assume that aviation and motoring meant the same thing; one can easily imagine some of its reactions upon Mr. Ford in his capacity of manufacturer and salesman. When he met with his associates in the trade, for example, he would have to talk more or less in terms of aviation, and cudgel his brains for ways to keep these conventional trade-terms in some kind of far-fetched correspondence with the actualities of motoring. *Absurd!* some one will say. Quite so; but not an iota more absurd than the reactions set up by the inveterate conventional confusion of re-publicanism with democracy, or of education with instruction. To prove it, listen to any campaign speech or to any commencement address; or read a copy of the *Congressional Record*, or the pro-ceedings of some gathering of pedagogues. If Mr. Henry Ford in-dulged in such inconsequent verbal antics before a group of his colleagues in the automobile industry, they would instantly ad-journ as one man and apply for a commission *de lunatico inquirendo*; and they would be quite right.

One great reason, perhaps the greatest, why Mr. Ford can speak with such certainty about his product, is that he has control of his raw material and can keep it up to standard quality. Now suppose that, in addition to the convention already named, there were a strong social convention whereby everybody assumed that any kind of material, good, bad, or indifferent, would make up into a satisfactory motor-car; suppose, even, that there were a law compelling Mr. Ford, at certain seasons of the year, to accept and use all the culls that the American Tin Plate Company chose to shovel in on him in the course of its regular consignments. What forecast could Mr. Ford make of his product? None, obviously; one car might run ten thousand miles, the next one a hundred, and the next might not live to get out of the shop. For the same reason, largely, our educational system is utterly unable to give any more than a very meagre, vague, and prayerful account of the product that it can turn out.

Moreover, under these circumstances Mr. Ford could not even be much more explicit about the kind of product that he *intended* to turn out than about the kind he *expected* to turn out. If the poor man decided that the motor-car business were worth going on with at all, he would bend his harassed mind to the problem of modifying his processes in order to bring his product up as near as possible to the specifications set by these two insane conventions. He would remodel his factory to produce out of the average run of his material something which would have all the talking-points of a flying-machine that he could put into it, consistently with making it able to get over the ground in some fashion or other. If the material in one car were above the average, the product would be no worse than hybrid; it would not fly at all, its pretences in this direction being only a decorative folly, and it would not run on land as well as if it had been made in a factory where production was geared to standard material only.

Here we have a pretty fair parallel, again, to the plight of our educational system. Everybody ought to go to school; everybody ought to go to college. The worth and respectability of an educational institution is popularly measured by the size of its "plant" and the number of its students. A big school is a great school. Every institution, therefore, has to have students; it has to have regard to their numbers only, not their quality — anything that will make an additional name on the register will do, for social convention has decreed the assumption that everybody possesses school-ability. By due obeisance to this set of conventions and its corollaries, our institutions grew mightily until they reached their present proportions and their present scale of expense.

But it was soon found that everybody did not have school-ability of more than a rudimentary type if even that. As the average of ability was watered down by the increased inflow of students, our educational system did just as we have supposed Mr. Ford might do under analogous conditions; it modified its processes so as to hit the least common denominator of ability in the material it dealt with. This modification was begun, as well as one can set a date to it, when the "elective system" was introduced at Harvard by the late President Eliot; who, in consequence, was enabled to ride the shoulders of American education like the Old Man of the Sea for nearly half a century, while the "elective system" which in principle is all very well for a university, made its way down into colleges and secondary schools — while, in short, education disappeared from among us, and instruction took its place. Before this period, as M. Renan said, America had indeed set up no serious higher education worth speaking of, but it had set up the beginnings, at least, of some serious primary education, and of a little secondary education; it now may quite fairly be said to have none of any kind. One should say this, too, as I do, without complaint; for what other measures of self-protection could our system take in the face of the dominant conventions? Executives like Mr. Butler and Mr. Eliot (I hope his admirers will forgive me for my plain speaking, for I too admire him as much as they) are great interpreters of the times; great educators, or, indeed, educators of any degree, they are not and never could be, and it is a disservice to them to obscure qualities worthy of all praise by a pretence that they are.

Those who regard my parallel between our educational system and Mr. Ford's enterprise as extravagant and far-fetched, might give me the benefit of a glance at the number and nature of the subjects taught in one representative secondary school, college, and university — I shall not suggest a choice, he may take his pick — and an estimate of the amount of brain-fag that an average mentality would suffer in "getting through" the minimum requirements laid down to cover a judicious selection from the bewildering list. I think he would cheerfully exonerate me. Consider one item only, the "courses in English." Some time ago, in table talk with one of the most highly cultivated men in America, we tried to make a rough estimate of the number of "courses in English" that are offered annually by our colleges and universities. It came to something like twenty thousand, to my great amazement; and from my own observation and experience, which circumstances have made a little larger than the average, perhaps, I should say that these courses are the last refuge of the incompetent and the idle, though this is by no means the same as saying that no others ever take them. Forty years ago, I believe, a course in English was practically unknown own among us; in the college I attended, back in the times of ignorance, such a thing was never dreamed of. Yet my fellow students managed somehow to write and speak pretty good English. On the other hand, I never yet had the pleasure of meeting a modern university graduate who had "specialized in English," who could either write English or speak English even tolerably. If my readers have had better luck, I congratulate them; I hope they have. Last year there fell under my hand a garland of literary windflowers culled from students by instructors, not in a primary school, not in a high school, not in a college, but in an American university, huge, prosperous, and flourishing. I do not know that the writers were "specializing in English"; but there they were, university students, and if one had not got one's eyeteeth cut, one might say they were therefore presumably literate, presumably intelligent. The following specimens bear testimony on these points:

"Being a tough hunk of meat, I passed up the steak."

"Lincoln's mind growed as his country kneaded it."

"The camel carries a water tank with him; he is also a rough rider and has four gates."

"As soon as music starts silence rains, but as soon as it stops it gets worse than ever."

"College students, as a general rule, like such readings that will take the least mental inertia."

"Modern dress is extreme and ought to be checked."

"Although the Irish are usually content with small jobs they have won a niche in the backbone of the country."

The instructor who reports these efforts also shows how Shakespeare fared at the hands of a group of sophomores and upper-classmen:

Edmund in "King Lear" "committed a base act and allowed his illegitimate father to see a forged letter." Cordelia's death "was the straw that broke the camel's back and killed the King." Lear's fool was prostrated on the neck of the

King." "Hotspur," averred a sophomore, "was a wild, irreso-
lute man. He loved honor above all. He would go out and
kill twenty Scotchmen before breakfast." Kate was a "woman
who had something to do with hot spurs".

Also Milton:

"Diabetes was Milton's s Italian friend," one student explained. Another said: "Satan had all the emotions of a
woman and was a sort of trustee in heaven, so to speak."
The theme of "Comus" was given as "purity protestriate."
Mammon in "Paradise Lost" suggests that the best way "to
endure hell is to raise hell and build a pavilion."

That will be about enough, I think. Let us ask ourselves once
more what Mr. Ford would do in like premises, and then rever-
ently take leave of the subject.

III

The third fundamental convention which besets our educational system is that by which we ignore the difference between
formative knowledge and instrumental knowledge; the convention whereby we assume that instrumental knowledge is all one
need have, that it will perfectly well do duty for formative knowledge; indeed, that it is in itself formative, as much so as any, and
that the claims heretofore made for the formative power of another type of knowledge were hierarchical and spurious. When
our system remodelled its processes to suit the requirements of
educational mass-production (speaking in industrial terms) our
educators began to talk a great deal about the need for our being
"men of our time," and taking on only such studies as "adapt us to
modern conditions" and "fit us to take our place in the present-
day world" — such studies, in short, as directly bear on the business of becoming chemists, engineers, bond-salesmen, lawyers,
horse-doctors, and so on. There was no direct relation superfi-
cially apparent between the type of study hitherto known as formative, and the actual practice of stock-jobbing, company-pro-
moting, or horse-doctoring; therefore this type of study could and

should be laid aside as a sheer waste of time and effort. Time was a great consideration, in fact, alike with students, parents, and a public that, as Bishop Butler says, was everywhere feverishly "impatient, and for precipitating things." The public ideal of excellence and success, generally speaking, was embodied in men who had themselves never been under the discipline of formative knowledge, and who neither wished nor were able to appraise that discipline intelligently for others. Our educational system at once rose to meet this attitude of the public — what else could it do? — and in the remodelling of its processes, formative studies either were flatly discarded or, when they went on at all, went on only in a vestigial fashion and under the blight of a general disregard and disparagement. At the present time even, as well as I am informed, our system has little or nothing to say about the relation of formative knowledge to the vocational practices of a really educated citizenry. Yet there is something to be said about it, and in view of the state of our society, about which most thoughtful observers have begun to be a little uneasy — a state resultant upon the unquestioned dominance of the conventions I have named — the subject seems worth reopening and reëxamining. President Butler of Columbia University was lately quoted by the newspapers as wondering why there are no longer any great men. The obvious rejoinder, of course, if one were ill-natured enough to make it, would be, How can there be any great men as long as Columbia University keeps on being what it is and doing what it does? The just rejoinder, however, is, How can there be any great men among us until the right relation between formative knowledge and instrumental knowledge becomes implicit in the actual practice and technique of education?

IV

While leading the world in mass-production, the United States also puts out a very slender and unconsidered line of quality-products that, as far as I know, are unequalled. The best suit of clothes I ever saw was made of an American homespun wool textile of which the entire annual output would not be enough, I dare say, to keep Hart, Schaffner & Marx busy fifteen minutes. Europe, the home of sausage, has nothing that can hold a candle to the Kingston sausage or the Lebanon County smoked sausage of Pennsylvania. The best shaving-cream, cologne-water, and mouth-wash I ever used are American, made more or less for the fun of the thing, apparently, by a very busy physician with a turn for chemistry, and if one can ever get them, one is lucky; I do not believe he takes time to make up a hundred dollars' worth of all three together in a year, so he almost never has any of them on hand. The best hard-water soap I ever saw — and, having an uncommonly thin skin, I have diligently tried many kinds, especially in our Lake regions, and Europe, where the water is as hard as Pharaoh's heart — is American, made as a side line by an old-time concern that does not seem to care whether it sells any of it or not; and hence the amount of search and supplication necessary to get it would be enough, probably, to reconcile a sinner to God, in a pinch. It is in the *average* of such matters, and many others that might be mentioned, that America ranks relatively low; and it is, of course, by the average that a country's production is to be judged. But the fact remains, as far as my experience goes, that in many lines America's quality-products, what little there is of them, and put out gingerly, almost surreptitiously, as they are, cannot be matched anywhere.

So it would seem that in a prosperous country of a hundred-odd million, where the mass-instructional system is wholly given over to the three conventions already cited, it might be possible to arouse some interest in a modest but very rigorous social experiment in quality-education, which should implacably defy those conventions. I have long had in mind a plan for such an experiment, in the shape of a strictly undergraduate college which should be limited to two hundred and fifty students. The only requirements for entrance should be (1) knowledge of arithmetic, and of algebra up to quadratics, (2) ability to read Greek and Latin, both prose and poetry, at sight, and to write Greek and Latin prose offhand. Nothing else, absolutely nothing, should be required, and any child worth educating can easily get up those requirements between the ages of eight and fifteen, if that is all he attempts to do. By reading Greek and Latin at sight and writing them offhand, I mean that when a boy entered this college, all language-difficulties, all the mechanical work with vocabulary and structure, be forever behind him, and he should be able to deal with Greek and Latin purely as literature.

The curriculum of the college should cover 1) the whole range of Greek and Roman literature, (2) mathematics up as far as the differential calculus, (3) late in the course, six or eight weeks work (three hours a week) in formal logic; and still later, the same amount of time on the *history* of the English language. Nothing but that; the college should pursue its mission as an educational experiment under the most jealously safeguarded aseptic experimental conditions, and it should be understood at the outset that the experiment could not be expected to yield anything approximating conclusive data for at least fifty years. There should be no "student activities" of any kind. The college should disallow and discourage any quasi-official relations with its alumni, and discountenance any representations from its alumni concerning its administration. When I went to college, the authorities regarded the alumni as little better than the scum of the earth, and there would have been joy in the presence of the angels on the day that the alumni barged in with suggestions about how the place should be run, or with attempts to cultivate "college spirit," and induce undergraduates to do and die for their dear old *alma mater*. You may believe there would. My recollections of the general atmosphere of that institution are very vivid; it was an atmosphere untainted with sentimentalism of any kind. The students regarded the instructors as their natural enemies, hated them manfully, and respected them immeasureably. Anything like a specious and sentimental Elk-Rotarian good-fellowship between professor and student, in those days, was undreamed of; and the thought of it would have been as much resented by the students, on the score of propriety, as by the faculty. It has never yet been clear to me that this state of things was unwholesome or undesirable.

The college I have in mind should have its experimental status established in such economic security that it need not care twopence whether any students ever came to it or not, or think twice about bouncing its whole undergraduate body, if need be. In fact, if such a college were set up tomorrow, probably not a single student would enter it for the first six or seven years, and if it had a baker's dozen at the end of ten years, I should be surprised. After that, I should expect it very soon to reach a capacity attendance; and if it stood fifty years without graduating more than fifty men, I believe its character as a social experiment would have been vindicated.

The theory of this college would be that if a young man wanted to go into engineering or horse-doctoring or selling bond he might prepare for it after he had got through this inflexible course at the age of twenty-one or so, with the degree of B.A., the only degree that this college should be empowered to confer, and it would be a degree, by the way, that amply meant what it pretended to mean, instead of meaning nothing, as it now mostly does. The test of this theory would be made by some impartial track being kept of these graduates, to see not only how they compared in a vocational way with men of another type of training, but how they stood in all-round ability, enlightenment, character, general culture, general good judgment, and good sense; how their views of life, their demands on life and their discernment of its values, compared with those of their contemporaries otherwise trained.

V

For the purposes of this little essay I am not interested in trying to forecast the results of this test, or to show reasons for stipulating these educational terms for it, because I am not here propounding a thesis, but only making a suggestion. If the suggestion takes root with any one who might wish to endow such an experiment, I should be glad to go into the subject with him to any length and quite disinterestedly, as I have no sort of ax to grind. Almost the last thing I would choose to be at my time of life is a college president, or a professor, or *Gott soll hutën*, a trustee. My interest is only in a competent diagnosis of the weaknesses and disabilities of American civilization — disabilities which are every day increasingly apparent — and in finding some remedy for them; and I believe that the social experiment I have outlined would throw enough light on both these matters to be worth its cost. With our educational system continually controlled by the conventions which now control it (and there is no prospect that I can see of its release), our civilization is likely to go on as it is. Argument *a priori* about the kind of civilization that might ensue upon an emancipation from these conventions would be as obviously futile and inert. Some line of practical approach, however, might be indicated *a posteriori*, by the experimental method, applied through such an institution as I have suggested; and in its essential features, as far as I am informed, there is not an institution in the United States today that remotely resembles the one I propose.

I discussed this idea at larger length lately with a young friend, a graduate of an English university, who wrote me as follows:

> But think of the poor devils who will have gone through your mill! It seems a cold-blooded thing, merely by way of experiment, to turn out a lot of people who simply can't live at home. Vivisection is nothing to it. As I understand your scheme, you are planning to breed a batch of cultivated, sensitive beings who would all die six months after they were exposed to your actual civilization. This is not Oxford superciliousness, I assure you, for things nowadays are precious little better with us. I agree with you that such spirits are the salt of the earth, and England used to make

some kind of place for them, not much, maybe, but there were backwaters where they could at least live and cooperate with their kind. But now — well, I hardly know. It seems as if some parts of the earth were jolly well salt-proof. The salt melts and disappears, and nothing comes of it.

This desponding sentiment may be sound or it may be unsound. But whatever one's opinion may be, I think that in spite of the chance of human sacrifice involved, an experiment tending towards something like actual evidence, one way or the other, would be greatly worth making.

Harper's – July, 1926

Concerning culture as a process, one would say that it means learning a great many things and then forgetting them; and the forgetting is as necessary as the learning.

THE VALUE OF USELESS KNOWLEDGE

I n conversation with a learned friend lately, our talk ran on various definitions of culture, and on the fact that for one reason or another we found them all unsatisfactory. This led us to ponder the notion that culture is one of those things that are perhaps better understood by not being too closely defined, like certain stars that become visible only when one looks a little away from them. We recalled the profound observation of Joubert, that "it is not hard to know God, provided one does not trouble oneself to define Him." There are many such matters, an astonishing number when one comes to count them up; astonishing, too, when one remarks how competent our working knowledge of them may be, notwithstanding our best definitions of them are so incompetent.

In regard to these matters, Truth shows herself the unscrupulous flirt that her devoted lover Ernest Renan finally declared her to be. A direct approach to her, a direct drive upon her coquettish reserve, is fatal to one's chances. A teasing wench, she lures one on by every charm, but at the moment one thinks to take her by force she slips out of one's grasp and is gone. Indeed, one never succeeds with her completely by any art of seduction; she is of the Rommany breed, and is bound to break one's heart at last, like Tchertapkhanov's gypsy, Masha. One must make up one's mind to that. But, again like Masha, each time one approaches her indirectly, tentatively, now by this side and now by that, never overpressing her coyness, she will make some little concession; and at the end of a lifetime of devotion one finds that the sum of her concessions is really considerable — not what one hoped for, certainly, but a fair reward, though platonic. One thankfully sorts them over and assembles them in terms of definition, though well aware that one's formulas are partial and provisional, and that one can never make them more than that.

II

It is perhaps only in this humble fashion that one may attempt a definition of culture; first of culture as a process, and then of culture as a possession. Concerning culture as a process, one would say that it means learning a great many things and then forgetting them; and the forgetting is as necessary as the learning. Diligent as one must be in learning, one must be as diligent in forgetting; otherwise the process is one of pedantry, not culture. The trouble with the pedant is not that be has learned too much, for one can never do that, but that he has not forgotten enough. In the view of culture, the human spirit is somewhat like the old-fashioned hectograph which had to be laid aside for a day or so after each use, to let the surface-impression sink down into the gelatine pad. The pedant's learning remains too long on the surface of his mind; it confuses and distorts succeeding impressions, thus aiding him only to give himself a conventional account of things, rather than leaving his consciousness free to penetrate as close as possible to their reality, and to see them as they actually are.

It would appear, though, that half the process of culture has been neglected in practice; or, worse than that, it has been disallowed and reprehended. Learning has always been made much of, but forgetting has always been deprecated; therefore pedantry has pretty well established itself throughout the modern world at the expense of culture. To cite perhaps the most conspicuous instances, it is no trouble to see how thoroughly pedantry has pervaded the world's practice of politics and economics. Nietzsche made the interesting observation that in the drama of politics the comic rôle has always been played by professors. This is very true, but when one considers the way in which the public affairs of most countries have been managed for the past two decades, one perceives that professors have no monopoly of pedantry. It is hard to believe that the drama of politics could have degenerated more swiftly and hopelessly into a roaring farce if the curtain had been rung up twenty years ago with nothing but professors in the cast. Pedantry pervades economics, dealing with them as it does with politics, by policies of sheer prestidigitation. The upshot of pedantry in politics is government by sleight-of-hand; its upshot in economics is a régime of extemporization. It can not be otherwise, because the essence of pedantry is to satisfy oneself wholly with a limited, partial and conventional account of things, then to assume that other people should and will satisfy themselves wholly with the same account, and then to become puzzled and indignant when it turns out that they do not.

The essence of culture is the exact opposite of all this; and here one may see where the importance of the second step in the process comes in. When the smart boy from the East Side or the farm-girl from the Mississippi Valley knocks at the gate of the college and declares for culture, one should say, "Youngster, this is a hard business that you are proposing, and a very long business. Are you sure it is what you want to undertake? Culture may not be quite what you think it is. The essence of culture is never to be satisfied with a conventional account of anything, no matter what, but always instinctively to cut through it and get as close as you can to the reality of the thing, and see it as it actually is. Culture's methods are those of exercising the consciousness in a free and disinterested play over any object presented to it, unchecked by prepossession and uncontrolled by formula. This exercise will keep you very busy for many years. In preparation for it, you must spend a great deal of time in learning a great many things, and then you must spend more or less time in forgetting them. Are you up to it? If you think you can manage the learning (for it must be actual learning — we shall see to that if you come here), what sort of fist do you think you can make at the forgetting? In any case, now that you have some idea of what it really is that you say you are after, does the thing strike you as worth trying? Do you believe you are equal to it?"

III

Our definition, however, is not quite explicit enough, because it does not specify the kind of knowledge that the process of culture contemplates. We all know that useful knowledge gains value by being remembered, and loses value by being forgotten; and it has most value when best remembered. Useless knowledge, on the contrary, gains value only as it is forgotten; and the point brought out is that useless knowledge alone is the concern of culture. Our definition, then, may be made more precise — perhaps as precise as any that can be made — if we put it that culture, considered as a process, means acquiring a vast deal of useless knowledge, and then forgetting it.

Perhaps the prevalence of pedantry may be largely accounted for by the common error of thinking that, because useful knowledge should be remembered, any kind of knowledge that is at all worth learning should be remembered too. By overlooking the fact that useless knowledge, if properly forgotten, has value, the common assumption is that the only kind of knowledge one should try to get is the kind that must be remembered. Here one has a crow to pick with the universities for promoting this error, for this is the ground of resentment against their wholesale adoption of ideals and methods that belong naturally and properly to the scientific school; and this too is the ground of particular resentment against their taking the scientific school into full partnership as a member of the academic organization. The university's undiscriminating attitude toward learning, its failure to establish a clear line between useful and useless knowledge, its misapprehension of values and its consequent misdirection of responsibility — all this the believer in culture is bound to regard as most unfortunate.

For *quid Athenis et Hierosolyma?* The business of a scientific school is the dissemination of useful knowledge, and this is a noble enterprise and indispensable withal; society can not exist unless it goes on. The university's business is the conservation of useless knowledge; and what the university itself apparently fails to see is that this enterprise is not only noble but indispensable as well, that society can not exist unless it goes on. The attitude of the university being what it is, one scarcely sees how the exceeding great value of useless knowledge is ever going to be properly appraised; and this is a hard prospect for the student of civilization to contemplate.

We all remember Mr. Stephen Leacock's account of his visit to Oxford, and his delightful portrayal of Oxford as the complete and perfect conservator of useless knowledge; a place where professors never lecture but by request, and then wretchedly, — Mr. Leacock was told that some had not lectured for thirty years, — where tutors seem to do nothing much but smoke, and students seem to do little but live in mouldy mediæval quarters, eat food cooked in Henry VIII's kitchen, and sleep in an unwholesome mess of age-old ivy. We recall his sly pretense of puzzlement when he compared the ways of Oxford with those of the universities that he was acquainted with on this side of the Atlantic, and finally his reluctant admission that somehow, dead against every conceivable possibility, Oxford "gets there," and his dark suspicion that it will continue to get there for many generations to come. No one in America knows the value of useless knowledge better than Mr. Leacock, and his fascinating sketch of Oxford makes it clear that the business of a university is to do what for centuries Oxford has been doing, and to turn out the kind of human produce that for centuries Oxford has been turning out.

But the traditional faculties of a university are those of Literature, Law, Theology, and Medicine; and by their professional side, the side first presented to the intending practitioner, the mastery of these subjects is a matter of science, a matter of absorbing much useful knowledge. True; but "the four learned professions" are very old, they have a long and heavily documented tradition, and in the course of their history they have laid all sorts and kinds of useless knowledge under continuous contribution, thus building up a thick accretion which, for the purposes of culture, is most valuable. It seems a fair question, then, whether the university should not occupy itself with this, and leave the professional side of the subjects to be dealt with by the scientific schools.

It seems fair to suggest, for example, that a true Faculty of Law at Harvard ought not to be equipping aspirants with useful knowledge in the way of getting up briefs, badgering witnesses, and steering flagitious enterprises with skill enough to keep their promoters out of jail. Let a good law-school do all that; the Faculty of Law should be taking on eligible products of the law-school, and filling them up bung-full of useless knowledge. In a word, the law-school should be producing sheer practitioners, giving them every chance at all the science, all the useful knowledge, that there is; the Faculty of Law should be producing practitioners like Sir Henry Maine, Maitland, Lord Penzance, or the Lord Chief Justice Coleridge. Let some medical school teach intending practitioners how to track down sinus-trouble and operate for appendicitis; the Faculty of Medicine at Johns Hopkins should be producing practitioners like William Osler, Mitchell, Draper, Pancoast, shoveling into them all the prodigious mass of useless knowledge that these men acquired, and then bidding them go forth and forget it as handily as these men did. There are enough divinity-schools in operation here and there to give students for the ministry all the useful knowledge necessary to a successful exercise of their profession. Let them attend to this, and meanwhile let the Faculty of Theology at Yale attend to its own business. If it did so, who knows but it might produce some theologians like the Cambridge Platonists, religious philosophers like Bishop Butler, moralists like the doctors of Salamanca? Things being as they are, we could do with a good many such just now, if we had them, and if we may not look to the university for them, where are we to look?

IV

So much, then, for culture when considered as a process. Considered now as a possession, one may define culture as the residuum of a large body of useless knowledge that has been well and truly forgotten. In order to see how this is so, let us take the simplest possible illustration. Let us suppose that I say to you, "Plato says so-and-so." You reply, "I think not. I can not speak positively, for I have long forgotten every word of Plato that I ever read. But all of Plato that I have read and forgotten, taken together with all I have read of a great many other authors and likewise forgotten, has left me with a clear residual impression that Plato never said anything like that." Then you look it up and find that you are right.

Being right about a saying of Plato is perhaps not important in itself, and this illustration must not be taken to imply that it is important. All this depends what the saying is, and the connexion in which it is brought forward. Plato said a great many fine things that are no doubt worth recalling on occasion, but the illustration is meant only to give a clearer notion of the kind of thing that a residuum of useless knowledge is, and how it works on the mind of the person who has it. The value of useless knowledge is another matter. I have already suggested that it has great value, and another type of illustration may serve to show in part what that value is. The field of useless knowledge is so vast that one might multiply illustrations almost indefinitely, and establish a tolerably complete set of values by their aid; but here, where there is no room for a treatise, we will keep to a single line of illustration, and a single line values.

The prime example of useless knowledge that occurs to me for this purpose is a knowledge of history. Alchemy, astrology, sociology, horoscopy — it is wildly conceivable that if one went in for any of these he might somewhere by some chance strike a trifling streak of "pay dirt"; whereas in the case of history such a thing is inconceivable, at least by me. Whether or not the best example, however, history seems to offer a very good example, as good as any I can bring to mind, of knowledge which is utterly useless except as it be forgotten; but which, when forgotten, becomes of great value. "The only thing that history teaches us," said the German philosopher, "is that history teaches us nothing"; and we may put the point of his epigram in still fewer words by saying merely that remembered history is valueless.

Let us suppose the case of one who, back in the bad old times when the university made a point of doing such jobs pretty thoroughly, had been loaded to the guards with history, perhaps by some Mommsen, Niebuhr or Guizot, and then turned loose to take the world as he found it. When he is well past middle age a war breaks out, and publicists, propagandists, pedants and professors lift up their voices with one accord to tell him that the cause of the war is absolutely this-or-that, the object of the war is absolutely thus-and-so, and that the character of one and another of the belligerents is absolutely such-and-such. If he has not forgotten his useless learning, if any of it remains on the surface of his mind, these affirmations encounter it and blend with it in a blur; and it is ten to one — nay, a hundred to one — that the account he gives himself of these matters, the account with which he finally satisfies himself will be as purely conventional as any of those that the pedants and propagandists offer.

But suppose his useless learning is gone. Life has obliged him to remember so much useful knowledge that he has lost not only his history, but his whole original cargo of useless knowledge; history, languages, literatures, the higher mathematics, or what you will — are all gone. The Carthaginian wars and the battle of Pavia are but names to him, or not even names. When they were fought, and where, and "how come," and who won, and why, and what the consequences were — of all this, or any of it, he knows nothing. All that aniline has sunk down into the hectograph pad, leaving no trace of a definite pattern; but it has diffused itself throughout the texture of the pad and imparted its colour to the gelatine. Therefore the affirmations of the pedants encounter no confusing surface-impressions, but encounter only a general cast of thought that has been coloured by purely residual learning. Hence he replies, "I think not. I think this war came about in quite another way, and that it has quite another set of objects"; and the mere passage of time brings proof that he is right.

Again, let us say that in the same circumstances an association of governments is proposed, to bring about permanent peace, to promote disarmament, to ensure the rights of racial minorities, to safeguard democracy, to protect small nations from molestation, and to further various laudable purposes. The proposal is taken up and vigorously pushed by energumens who declare that this association is meant to do all these things and will unfailingly do them. The man who has forgotten all his useless learning was once aware that this proposal would be nothing new, that similar associations similarly advertised have already appeared in history under similar circumstances; but now he remembers nothing about any of them, not even its name. He says, however, "No, I believe this association is proposed for quite different purposes, and that it will never accomplish any of the things you say it will"; and, again, the mere passage of time proves that he is right. It may appear, indeed he himself may think, that his reaction is instinctive, but it is not; it is due to the residuum of useless and forgotten learning.

Thus it may be seen how useless knowledge can be made directly contributory to a force of sound and disinterested public opinion. We are told nowadays that such opinion will never prevail in a republic, and indeed, as things stand, it seems unlikely to do so; if for no other reason, because it is inimical to well-established political interests, and to the general auspices under which public affairs are managed. The business of a practical politician, as Edmund Burke said, is "still further to contract the narrowness of men's ideas, to confirm inveterate prejudices, to inflame vulgar passions, and to abet all sorts of popular absurdities." He is all for the theory that moral questions are determinable by a plebiscite; that right and wrong, truth and falsehood, come down in the last instance to a matter of counting noses, and therefore their practical test is always, as we say, "what one can get away with." This being so obviously the case, there is small chance that a force of sound and disinterested public opinion can prevail. Nevertheless it is generally thought desirable that such a force should exist in society, and, if that be so, any discipline likely to "generate it must be regarded as valuable.

The discipline of useless knowledge, moreover, moves a person always to "run to the short way" in his estimate of public enterprises, to strike through to their first principles and "the reason of the thing," instead of being caught and held by their more manifest aspects. When someone tells him, for example, what a good thing for Rome it was to win the Carthaginian wars, cabbage all the trade of Carthage, and set up a great Mediterranean empire, he replies that it was certainly impressive, but, as to its being a good thing for Rome, he would first have to know what the Romans were like when they got through doing it. Thus he cuts straight through to the first principle so often cited by Mr. Jefferson, that a public enterprise is to be judged, not by its direct effect on commerce, finance, industry, employment and the like, but by its effect on collective human character; and a discipline which moves him invariably to judge it in this way has value.

V

We hear on all sides that the world is in a bad way, so bad as to give but slim assurance that anything worth doing can be done about it. Some think we are plunging into the chaos of the Dark Ages; others think we are at the end of an era, and entering into a new mediævalism. One suspects that these views of our situation may be a little excessive, or at least that while waiting for the crash we have time to be cheerful. If it be true, however, that the world is actually perishing before our eyes, there is perhaps some sort of melancholy interest in the thought that it may be perishing largely of inattention to the value of useless knowledge.

Nothing shows more clearly how profound this inattention is than the nature of current comment on the New Deal. This comment runs to millions of words, and covers every conceivable question suggested by our public enterprises except the one that the man of forgotten learning most wants to hear discussed. He is naturally interested in the outcome of these enterprises, interested to see how the American variant of Statism and corporalism is going to work, and therefore he is glad to read all the intelligent comment on it, pro and con, that comes his way; but the previous question always rises in his mind. Suppose our adventure in Statism works perfectly, suppose the New Deal scores a clean success at every practical point, what kind of people are we going to be when it has done so?

This, in his view, is the really important question raised by the recrudescence of Statism in Europe. He is aware that Bolshevism, Fascism, Hitlerism, are all essentially identical, all branches off the same tree planted by the German idealist philosophers in the early years of the last century. They all mean, in essence, that the State is everything, the individual nothing. Fichte put it that "the State is the superior power, ultimate and beyond appeal, absolutely independent," and Hegel said that "the State is the general substance, whereof individuals are but accidents." There is the general formula for all variants of the common doctrine of Statism.[1] Well, then, what one really wants to know is the effect

---

[1] This seems to be officially acknowledged. Compare this formula with Mussolini's declaration that "the State embraces everything, and nothing outside the State has value. The State creates right"; with Hitler's assertion that "the State dominates the nation because it alone represents it"; and with Lenin's frank admission that "it is nonsense to make any pretense of reconciling the State and liberty."

that this doctrine is likely to produce in the long run upon the character of those who swallow it. In the long run, what will Mussolini's Italians be like, or Hitler's Germans, or Stalin's Russians?

Certain features of the American variant of Statism raise the same question about ourselves, but they are never discussed; one never hears anything about them. They are four in number: first, according to Mr. Hopkins's report published on the day I write this, thirty million persons, nearly one-fourth of our population, are being subsidized by the Federal Government; second, a vote-controlling bureaucracy has been prodigiously expanded; third, executive control over legislation has been made almost absolute through the distribution of money in the Congressional districts; fourth, centralization has been made almost absolute by federal grants to the states, or, as one writer puts it very well, these subsidies have set up a carpetbag government in every state.

These features of the New Deal impress the man of forgotten learning so unfavorably that he gets out his dusty books and looks up his history to see if perchance he may be wrong; and he finds that he is not wrong. His impression is abundantly made good. Curiously, too, the instance that most conspicuously corroborates it is one where no blame, no disparagement, no breath of suspicion, could rightfully be directed against the executive authority, but quite the opposite; and this pleases him, because he likes to consider all such matters, or indeed all matters, as impersonally as possible.

At the end of the first century, Rome had already seen how easily a republic slides off into a despotism, and despotism into ruinous tyranny. Things had been at low tide in the empire for some time; the Flavian dynasty had petered out to the tune of something that one could really call a depression. Meanwhile mendicancy and subvention had been erected into a permanent political asset, not at first embracing one fourth of Rome's population, probably, but well on its way to do so. Bureaucracy, which in earlier times hardly counted, began to spread wide and grow rapidly. Centralization busily undermined the large measure of self-rule that had prevailed in the provinces and even more largely in the cities. Quite in the tone of Mr. Jefferson, Plutarch speaks bitterly of this decay of local public spirit, saying that those who refer every two-penny detail of public life to Rome must share the spiritual fate of the hypochondriac who will neither bathe nor eat but as the doctor tells him.

Then a remarkable thing happened. For the next eighty years the empire was governed by an unbroken succession of extraordinarily able and good rulers, each one better than his predecessor. The short and good reign of Nerva bridged the turn of the century. Then came Trajan, the most just, frugal and energetic of all Rome's emperors, so far. Then Hadrian, who added to Trajan's virtues great wisdom and foresight, breadth of view, and range of sympathy. Then Antoninus Pius, whom to name is enough, and then one who need not even be named; the world has not once looked upon his like, and his praise is for ever and ever. Yet hardly was the breath out of his body before the rotten social fabric of Rome disintegrated, and the empire crumbled to pieces.

If ever rulers were disinterested, these were. None of them wished to set up a carpetbag government in the provinces and cities. They clearly foresaw the upshot of organized mendicancy and subvention, of the growing power of bureaucracy, of the growing tendency to centralization. They did the best they could to check these malignant growths, but could do nothing. The combination of job-holders, prætorian guards, frontier soldiers and subsidized Roman rabble could turn out any disobliging government on short notice by the simple expedient of cutting a disobliging emperor's throat. The mere suspicion that Nerva was for a general policy of retrenchment brought sudden fate on him, and even Trajan, the most heavy-handed of the lot, could do little worth doing in the way of reform. The emperors of the second century remind one of nothing so much as an array of the world's best physicians striving to reclaim a hopeless cancer-patient.

The thing could not be done; there is the whole story. The cancer of organized mendicancy, subvention, bureaucracy and centralization had so far weakened its host that at the death of Marcus Aurelius there was simply not enough producing-power left to pay the bills. Under the exactions of the job-holders, nobody could do any business, fields went untilled, and even the army had to be recruited among foreigners. But to the man of useless learning these matters are only relatively important. In his view the significant thing is that, under the conditions existing, eighty years of continuous effort by five of the world's best and ablest rulers could not prevent the Roman populace from degenerating into the very scum of the earth, worthless, vicious, contemptible, sheer human sculch.

A rather long-winded illustration, possibly, in support of my thesis that useless knowledge has value, but the fact that no one else is saying anything on the subject may perhaps serve as its excuse.

Brussels, December, 1933
Atlantic Monthly – May, 1934

---------------- ⊗ ----------------

*We insist that civilization is not to be measured in
terms of longevity, trackage, the abundance of banks
and newspapers, the speed and frequency of mails,
and the like. Civilization is the progressive
humanization of men in society . . .*

---------------- ⊗ ----------------

TOADSTOOLS

In one of his earlier books Mark Twain tells of seeing a toad-stool which in its growth had dislodged and pushed up into the air a mass of tangled roots and leaves, amounting to twice its own bulk. Commenting on this display of strength, he says: "Ten thousand toadstools with the right purchase could lift a man, I suppose. But what good would it do?"

There should be more of this strong common sense employed to make our estimate of our civilization less formal and more fundamental. One of the most striking differences between the Oriental mind and ours is seen here. The Oriental is struck with our way of regarding things and actions as good in themselves, without reference to individual and personal realization; and it seems strange and unnatural to him. Railways, banks, telephones, finance-companies, industrial development, newspapers — all such things are most commonly and generally accepted among us as absolute goods in themselves, quite irrespective of their effect upon the spirit of the individual life, and the quality of the collective life, which are lived under their influence. Let a new railway be laid out, or the postal service be increased, or some new device be invented for quickening communication or transportation, and our general tendency is to accept it at once without question as a good thing, not considering that its whole value is to be measured by its effect upon the spirit and quality of life, and that until this effect be ascertained our estimate of it is worthless and misleading. Our newspapers teach us to take this formal and mechanical view of trade-balances and the expansion of industry, never raising the question whether these actually tend towards a better spirit and finer quality of human life or whether they tend towards a spiritual impoverishment and vulgarization; nor is it regularly pointed out that unless they are so employed as progressively to improve life, unless they are practically interpreted in terms of personal realization, they are hardly worth having.

Surely common sense and the free play of consciousness upon the facts of the material world about us are enough to show that this formal view, almost universal as it is, is superficial and retarding. We read the other day a complaint from a railway-official about new trackage. It seems that only a few miles of new trackage have been laid during the past year. He spoke of this as a calamity, as indeed it may be, but the mere fact does not prove itself as such. One must go further and ask whether it can be shown that individual realization has at all profited, and if so how much, by what trackage we already have. How does the spirit of American life compare, indeed, with the spirit of life at a period when there was no trackage at all? Again, we read not long ago a statement by the president of a great chemical concern, in which he predicted that science would possibly before long enable us to produce synthetic food, cheap fuel, artificial wool; to store solar heat, to do without sleep and to prolong mental and physical vigour. The tone of the statement left no doubt that this chemist regarded all these matters as absolute goods in themselves, whereas clearly they are nothing of the kind. If they are made to tend towards the enrichment and deepening of the spiritual life of man, they will be good; if they are made to tend against it, they will be bad; if they are made to tend neither way, they are of no consequence except in point of curiosity, like Mark Twain's toadstool.

Again, we lately saw the advertisement of a life-extension institute, headed, "Do You Want to Add Ten Years to Your Life?" Here once more the obvious assumption was that longevity is in itself a good and desirable thing. But is it? There is of course in all of us the primary instinct of self-preservation which speaks out strongly in favour of living as long as we can; and it is to this instinct, this irrational and almost bloodthirsty clinging to life, that the advertisement was intended to appeal. As such it seemed to us, we admit, a little ignoble; we were reminded, as all such enterprises which are now so much in vogue remind us, of Julius Cæsar's remark that life is not worth having at the expense of an ignoble solicitude about it. But instinct apart, the worth of such enterprises is measured, surely, by the quality of the life which we are invited to prolong. The content of the average life being what it is, and its prospects of spiritual enlargement and enrichment being what they are, may longevity be so indubitably regarded as an absolute good that one is justified in an almost ferocious effort to attain it?

We are not now concerned that these questions be answered; we are concerned only that they be raised. We are concerned with the habit, which seems to us unintelligent and vicious, of regarding potential accessories to civilization as essential elements in civilization. We insist that civilization is not to be measured in terms of longevity, trackage, the abundance of banks and newspapers, the speed and frequency of mails, and the like. Civilization is the progressive humanization of men in society, and all these things may or may not sustain a helpful relation to the process. At certain periods and places, indeed, the process has been carried notably further without any of them than it is now carried with all of them. When we learn to regard them intelligently, when we persuade ourselves that their benefit is potential and relative, not actual and absolute, then we are in the way of intelligently and quickly applying them to the furtherance of true civilization; but as long as we unintelligently regard them as absolute goods in themselves, we shall merely fumble with them.

Freeman – December, 1923

---

*. . . our militant feminists are reduced to pushing
minor issues, to smoothing out relatively petty
inequalities . . . the more progressive and thoughtful
spirits among our feminists should consider the thesis
that women can do something men can not do. Women
can civilize a society, and men can not.*

A Word to Women

A long time ago — all of three years, perhaps longer — I saw a floating item in a periodical to the effect that forty-one per cent of our national wealth is controlled by women, and that the percentage is rising. Curiously, this bit of news did not make much of an impression on me at the time, but the recollection of it kept coming back to me afterward, and more frequently as time went on. After being pestered in this way for three years or more, I bethought myself of an acquaintance who has facilities for looking up data on such matters, and asked him to get chapter and verse for me, which he very kindly did.

It appears that a firm of investment bankers operating in Chicago and New York had made an investigation into the division of our national wealth between the sexes. They did this purely in the way of business, of course, to determine the amount of stress that could profitably be laid on female clientage. The general conclusion was that at the time the survey was made, say four years ago, nearly half our national wealth was controlled by women, and that the proportion was tending to increase steadily and rather rapidly. Some of the incidental findings turned up by the investigation are interesting. It found that ninety-five billion dollars' worth of life-insurance policies were in force in this country, and that eighty per cent of their beneficiaries were women. This alone would considerably help along the rising proportion of female control, unless there were somewhere some offset which the survey did not show. An even more interesting finding is that by wills probated in New York City, over a given period, fifty estates out of seventy were left by men to women, and forty-four out of sixty-nine were left by women to women. It found that women were taxed on three and a quarter billion dollars of income annually; men, on four and three quarters. One hundred and thirty-nine women paid taxes on incomes in excess of a half million, as against one hundred and twenty-three men; while forty-four women paid on net incomes in excess of a million, as against forty-two men. Women were found to be majority or almost majority shareholders in some of our largest corporations, for instance the Pennsylvania Railway, American Telephone and Telegraph, United States Steel, Westinghouse Air Brake and National Biscuit Company.

It should be remembered, too, that American women have a good deal more purchasing-power than this survey shows, because many of those who legally own nothing are on fairly liberal allowances from male members of their families, and many more are wage-earners who spend their wages as they please. Women's collective virtual control is thus considerably larger than their legal ownership indicates. This surplus of petty wage-earning and of what might be called delegated control is not a matter of interest to investment bankers, so the survey did not attempt to take account of it; yet its aggregate must be quite large. There seems little ground for doubt that, taking virtual control with legal control, our women now have more purchasing-power than our men have. Four years ago they were within nine per cent of equality in legal control, and quite rapidly on the rise; and surely the amount of delegated control which they exercise, plus their wage-earnings, would be enough to carry the sum of their purchasing-power well over the mark of fifty per cent.

II

In Europe one notices a general prevalence of the notion that our country is a paradise for womankind. Europeans think we operate our institutions greatly to the advantage of the female sex. Some years ago a highly placed English dignitary — I think it was the present Dean of St. Paul's — spoke of the United States as "an ice-water-drinking gynecocracy." The popular idea on the Continent appears to be that our women do as they please without let or hindrance, and that they have reduced our men to the Levitical status of hewers of wood and drawers of water, if not to that of mere skulkers upon the face of the earth. Continental women — those, at least, with whom I am acquainted — indulge this notion with interested curiosity, in which one sometimes discerns a touch of envy. A more conservative opinion is that, while our women have managed to gain an unshakable ascendancy, they have also managed to establish a roughly satisfactory relation of live-and-let-live with their male entourage, mostly by way of concession, which is not as a rule too onerous and not perhaps utterly degrading; a relation, however, which, with all the good will in the world, a male European would find hard and repugnant.

The wonderment is, how the American woman has done it. This more than anything, I think, is what has always made our women an object of special interest to the European mind. I never saw anything to make me suspect that Europeans of either sex like our womenfolk or admire them especially or even much respect them, but they have always showed great curiosity about them, somewhat like our curiosity about the habits of the sea-bear or the peculiarities of the lemming, or the traits in other creatures whose main interest for us is that they keep us wondering how they accomplish what they do, and do it apparently with no great fuss or effort, nor any consciousness that they are doing something unusual and striking.

One sees Europeans regarding casual specimens of our petticoated produce, more often than not pretty poor specimens, and wondering what on earth they have in them to have worked themselves into their highly privileged status, and to have got this status accepted without objection or complaint. The European would say that such a notable collective manœuvre betokens first-rate ability somewhere, and he can not see that they have it; his own womenfolk, by and large, seem much abler, wiser, more mature of mind. Cleverness will not answer; he acknowledges that American women are very clever, but no one can be *that* clever. Nor can such a piece of strategy be put through nationwide on the strength of feminine fascinations, even granting that American women are endowed with these beyond all other women, which he thinks highly doubtful. All the horde of foreign "observers," novelists, dramatists, journalists, lecturers and the like, who beset our shores, usually with some sort of axe to grind, always show that this problem is in the forefront of their minds. They treat it with gingerly deftness, as a rule, and hence their observations are seldom valuable, but they always exhibit a lively curiosity about it.

The best that European opinion has done with this problem, as far as I know, amounts to saying more or less kindly that our women are shockingly spoiled and that our men spoil them. In its view the American man of family appears, by his serious side, as a kind of composite of Silas Lapham and Mr. Potiphar. By his lighter side, he appears when on parade with his frolicsome daughter (or wife or sister, as the case may be) much as he does in Mr. Georges Lauwerijns's utterly delightful ballet called *Hopjes and Hopjes*, which anyone going to Brussels should time his visit to see and hear. European opinion holds what it regards as our men's weakness, their easy-going good nature, their sense of essential inferiority, responsible for letting themselves be choused out of their natural and Scriptural rights over the women of their households.

There is something in this, of course, and there was formerly much more in it than there is now. Mr. Potiphar and Silas Lapham are real enough, but they belong to an earlier day. Mr. Lauwerijns's figures are modern and not greatly exaggerated — the simple-hearted and likable old boy who never learned how to play, out on a lark with his gay daughter who is rather fond of him in her careless fashion, is on good terms with him, and exploits him scandalously. Mr. Sinclair Lewis has perhaps a little over-vulgarized a somewhat similar pair, in his excellent portrait of Mr. Lowell Schmaltz and his daughter Delmerine. But there is no longer any point in discussing the distribution of responsibility. In cuing, the American man's traditional easiness with women, European opinion may have had everything on its side in the days of Daisy Miller, and may still have something on its side. What it has or has not, however, is no longer of more than academic interest, because a new factor has come into the situation since Silas Lapham's and Daisy Miller's day — the factor of economic control. It may be said, no doubt, that men were culpably shortsighted not to foresee this factor's coming in and to take measures against it; but that is little to the point now, because the mischief, if mischief it be, is done, and there is no help for it.

The thing now, I take it, is to measure the strength of this new factor, and to observe some of its bearings. I venture to suggest this because no one, as far as I know, has ever taken the American woman's proportion of ownership and her probable preponderance of purchasing-power into account as affecting her freedom of action, and as in consequence putting certain definite marks upon our society which do not appear on any other. I am no such hidebound disciple of the Manchester school as to pretend that the American woman's position is to be accounted for in economic terms alone. I say only that her economic status has a great deal to do with defining and establishing her social status, her social privileges and immunities, and that in this relation her economic status has never, as far as I am aware, been competently considered by any critic, native or foreign; and since one short essay will hardly go around the whole subject, it may properly devote itself to this single aspect of it, even at the risk of appearing limited and partial.

III

To-day processes the refractory raw material of yesterday's heresy into the standard tissue of orthodoxy; and to-morrow re-processes its remnants into the shoddy of commonplace. Side by side with this procedure, and apparently related to it, go odd changes of fashion concerning delicacy and indelicacy of speech. A dozen years ago, it was most indecorous to say anything suggesting the doctrine that those who own rule, and rule because they own. We all knew that the doctrine was sound, but, like a sound doctrine of certain biological functions, there was a convention against speaking of it, above all against letting anything about it appear in print. The correct thing was to say that those who vote rule, and rule because they vote — standard eighteenth-century political theory. The fashion has changed now, and everybody speaks quite freely of the relation between ownership and rulership. Even our more progressive institutions of learning no longer make any difficulties about the fact that actual rulership of a population rests finally in the control of its means of livelihood, and that this is vested in ownership.

Our government "buys," we say, an island from a foreign government. One flag is hauled down, another is hauled up; one set of officeholders decamps, another comes in. But the island is actually owned by three men and the same three men who owned it under the foreign government continue to own it under ours. They are the actual rulers of the island's population, because they can make it do what they please, — which is the essence of rulership, — since they control the source of its livelihood. Some years ago a Greenbacker or free-silverite, I forget which, discussing private land-monopoly with Henry George, said, "Give me all the money in the world, and you may have all the land." "Very well," said George, "but suppose I told you to give me all your money or get off — what then?"

Ownership means the ability to make people obey your will under the implicit menace of shutting off their supplies, or what we call in war-time an economic blockade. I do not suggest this as an academic definition, but we all know that it is what ownership comes to. It seems clear, therefore, that the distinctive character of a preponderating ownership would be pretty faithfully reflected by the society in which that ownership was exercised. Hence, when Europeans regard our society as deeply effeminized and wonder why it should be so, the most competent answer, surely, is found in the amount of economic control that is in our women's hands. How it got there is of no present consequence; it is there, and apparently there to stay. How is it possible for a society not to be effeminized when its women have so large a power of imposing upon it their collective will, of impressing upon it the distinctive mark of their collective character, their criteria of intelligence, taste, and style?

I suspect that the extent to which women direct our national development in the realm of the spirit is quite imperfectly realized. Putting it bluntly, they control education, they control the church, the forum, publishing, drama, music, painting, sculpture. That is to say, in the United States the musical director, preacher, publisher, lecturer, editor, playwright, schoolmaster, always instinctively addresses himself to the quality and character of interest peculiar to the female portion of his constituency. In Europe he is under no pressure to do so. In fact, this is the most noticeable difference between the practice of these activities here and in Europe, and I think the most significant as well. It is surely more than a coincidence that the increase of women's control of our practice has gone on in a fairly direct ratio to their increase in purchasing-power. A study of woman's rise to her present position discloses too many such coincidences for us to take stock in the presumption of coincidence. Her demand for political equality, for instance, was pushed hard and earnestly for nearly a century, but one observes with interest that nothing came of it until the time, almost to the day, that she arrived at equality in purchasing-power; and then she got what she wanted with relatively little effort.

Now, in any society, the status of the pursuits I have just mentioned, the status of what goes on in the realm of the spirit, is the measure of that society's actual civilization. Exercise of the instinct of workmanship alone, no matter how energetic, is not civilizing; there must go on with it a balanced and harmonious exercise of the instinct of intellect and knowledge, of religion and morals, of beauty and poetry, of social life and manners. A society may be very rich, it may have any number of industries, railways, hygiene-establishments, sport-centres, banks, newspapers, telephones, finance-companies and the like, and remain quite uncivilized. These things are in a sense the apparatus of civilization, because under proper direction they make for a diffused material well-being, and civilization can get on better if it has this as a basis; but they do not in themselves constitute civilization or even make directly and immediately toward it.

IV

My main design in writing this essay is to address a word of exhortation to our feminists. Modern feminism has contented itself with asserting the thesis of women's ability and right to do everything that men can do. Perhaps some of our more thoughtful feminists have looked beyond this thesis, but I know of none, from the days of Fanny Wright and Susan B. Anthony on to the present, who has done so. Feminism has been content with demanding the right to vote, to practise politics and hold public office, as men do, and to enter commerce, finance, the learned professions and the trades, on equal terms with men, and to share men's social privileges and immunities on equal terms. Its contention is that women are able to do as well with all these activities as men can do, and that the opportunity to engage in them is theirs by natural right.

This thesis is wholly sound. Every objection I ever heard raised against it has impressed me as *ex parte* and specious — in a word, as disingenuous. There is no doubt whatever that women can do everything that men can do: they have always done it. In the thirteenth century, women were not only studying and practising, but also lecturing, in the Faculty of Medicine at the University of Salerno. Joan of Arc made no special impression on the people of France as a military figure; they were quite used to seeing women under arms in the mediæval wars. As late as the sixteenth century, Louise Labé got a bit bored with the routine life of a well-to-do merchant's daughter at Lyon, so she reached down the gun, sallied forth in men's dress, and fought through the siege of Perpignan. Then, having had her little fling at an active outdoor life, she went back to Lyon, married, and made her home the centre of a brilliant literary society, and wrote some of the most beautiful verse ever done in the French language, or, for that matter, in any language. She also wrote an excellent manual of housekeeping in a practical and sententious style rather reminding one of Cato's treatise; which seems to show that she was quite as handy with the broom and rolling-pin as she was with the pen and the smooth-bore.

Then, as a type of the first-class executive and diplomat, there was Saint Radegonde, in the sixth century. Our feminists ought to look her up as the patron saint of feminism, and I say no more about her in the hope that they will do so; she will be a rich find for them. In the realm of public affairs, the women of the French and Italian Renaissance are too well known to need mention. Even the gun-moll, generally supposed to be a product peculiar to our time and country, has a very early prototype. In the sixth century two spirited hussies, mere youngsters, princesses named Chrodhilde and Basine, pranced out of Saint Radegonde's convent at Poitiers in dudgeon against the management, gathered a band of cutthroats around them, and shot the town to rags. The streets of Poitiers ran red with blood, and the forces of law and order had a frightful time putting down the riot. Indeed, the two princesses never were put down. They rode off somewhere beyond the reach of extradition — some mediæval Miami, probably — and lived to a green old age, full of ginger, and wearing the halo of popular renown. That was many centuries ago, but even to this day the Nuns' War is mentioned with uneasy respect throughout the Poitou.

At any period in history, I think, one may find women "living their own lives" in the feminists' sense, about as satisfactorily as men were living theirs; doing, if they chose, just what men did, and doing it just about as well. One must observe, however, that these women were relatively few, they were always exceptional, and — here is, I think, the important thing — they were all marked by one sole invariable differentiation: they were economically independent. I say "all" rather inadvisedly, perhaps, for I have not looked into the pocketbooks of all the notable women in the world, from Semiramis down; but out of curiosity I have lately examined the circumstances of a great many, here and there, and have found but one exception, Joan of Arc. She was a poor girl; but her enterprise was of a very special kind, not likely to be affected by her economic status, though if she had been well-to-do she might not, quite probably would not, have lost her life in the way she did. Given a certain amount of resolution, women who were economically independent seem never to have had much trouble about "living their own lives"; nor, apparently, do they now.

It may therefore be said, I think, that the efforts of feminism have never been, strictly speaking, in behalf of the rights of women, but in behalf of the rights of poor women; and all the greater honour to feminism that this is so! Those who were not poor or dependent seem always to have been able pretty well to do as they liked with themselves, and, as our expressive slang goes, "to get away with it." It must be remarked that, for our present purposes, the wage-earning woman is not to be classed as economically independent, for she holds her place on sufferance of an employer. By economically independent, I mean those who are fixed quite securely in the owning class, as were the eminent women of the Renaissance, for instance.

It would appear, however, that feminism in America has not many more fish to fry in the way of its historic contention. If our women of the owning class very much want anything, they are able to concentrate upon it an amount of purchasing-power which constitutes an economic demand hardly to be resisted; and their getting it would be likely to accrue to the benefit, if it were a benefit, of the dependent members of their sex as well. A rather trivial instance of this is seen in the latter-day style of dress. We remember that when women took to the wholesome fashion of wearing almost no clothes at all, especially on our beaches in summer, all the institutional voices of our society spoke out against them. The police and our prurient and officious local Dogberrys made trouble for them, and employers held a blanket threat of dismissal over the head of girls who would not conform to more conservative notions of propriety in dress. But there was enough purchasing-power concentrated on the style to hold it in force and to bring all objectors to terms; and the poor and dependent women profited accordingly. Putting it broadly, Fourteenth Street could not have held up the style, but Park Avenue could and did, and Fourteenth Street shared the benefit.

Hence feminism can no longer get up an argument on the thesis that women can do anything that men can do. All interest in that contention has died out; everybody has stopped thinking in those terms, and our militant feminists are reduced to pushing minor issues, to smoothing out relatively petty inequalities of legal status, and the like. This is important and should be done; but I suggest that while it is being done the more progressive and thoughtful spirits among our feminists should consider the thesis that women can do something which men can not do.

V

Women can civilize a society, and men can not. There is, at least, no record that men have ever succeeded in civilizing a society, or even that they have made a strong collective endeavour in this direction; and this raises a considerable presumption upon their inability to do either. They can create the apparatus of a civilization, the mechanics of that diffused material well-being upon which a civilization is founded. Men are good at that; they are first-rate at founding industries, building railways, starting banks, getting out newspapers, and all that sort of thing. But there is no record of their handiness at employing this apparatus for a distinctly civilizing purpose. Indeed, it is very doubtful whether, left strictly to themselves, they would employ the greater part of it, the part that bears on what we call the amenities of life, for any purpose; they would incline to let it drop out of use. The standard cartoons and jokes on the subject all tend to show that when the missus goes away for the summer, the gent lapses contentedly into squalor and glories in his shame; and these may be taken as an allegory reflecting matters of larger consequence.

In the greater concerns of life it is the absence of the impulse toward civilization that justifies women in their complaint that men are forever children. Men feel no more natural, unprompted sense of responsibility than children feel, for the work of civilizing the society in which they find themselves; hence in respect of all life's concerns, even its very greatest, women have been figuratively cuffing and coaxing this sense into their heads, figuratively overhauling them, not so much for unwashed ears and unblown noses as for the persistent *tendency* toward these, the indefeasible disposition to accept a general régime of unwashed ears as normal and congenial, and to regard any complaint of it as exorbitant.

A while ago I took occasion to write something which bore on this point, and it elicited a very tart letter from a lady, asking me what I meant by "civilizing a society." I have no notion that the letter was written in good faith; still, the question is a fair one. Words, as Homer says, "may tend this way or that way," and nothing is ever lost by making sure that one's use of terms is always perfectly clear. We have already mentioned mankind's five fundamental social instincts — the instinct of workmanship, of intellect and knowledge, of religion and morals, of beauty and poetry, of social life and manners. A civilized society is one which organizes a full collective expression of all these instincts, and which so regulates this expression as to permit no predominance of one or more of them at the expense of the rest; in short, one which keeps this expression in continual harmony and balance.

To civilize a society, then, means that when this harmony is imperfect, when the expression of one or more of these instincts is over-stressed, the civilizing force should throw its weight in favour of the under-expressed instincts and steadily check the over-stress on the others, until a general balance is restored. Social development under these conditions is, properly speaking, a civilized development; and a civilized person is one who manages the expression of his individual five instincts in just this way, and directs himself into just this course of orderly individual development.

Men have, of course, managed this individual development in themselves; though even here, unfortunately, it is seldom clear what part a distinctly feminine influence has played in its direction. Men apparently, however, have neither the ability nor the aptitude to organize and direct a collective development of the kind; and women seem to have both. Men's collective influence has never, that I can discover, even tended significantly in this direction; women's often has. It would therefore appear as certain as any generalization can be that, while women can do everything that men can do, they can also do this one thing that men can not do: they can civilize a society.

The correspondent whom I mentioned a moment ago intimated that in my interest in this matter I was entertaining myself with a mere logomachy, and that my reflections upon it were all moonshine. In a personal view, one does not mind this; one should be always glad of criticism, just or unjust. But the personal view is unimportant. The important thing is to observe that in the long course of human experience, whenever a society has gone on the rocks, as sooner or later all have done, it was invariably the collective over-stress on one or more of these fundamental instincts that turned it out of its course and wrecked it. One may look back upon any of these societies, — England of the Commonwealth, France of the *Grand Siècle*, any you please, — identify at once the over-stressed and the neglected instincts, and follow through the record of progressive over-stress and progressive repression, running directly on to final disaster. Similarly, one may work out the prospects of an existing society with almost actuarial exactness by observation of these symptoms, as critics have often done. Hence one is concerned with the degree of civilization attained by the society in which one lives, not on such grounds as my correspondent might regard as more or less fanciful, but upon the solid ground of security. An uncivilized society has in it the seeds of dissolution, it is insecure; and the lower the degree of its civilization, as measured by the means I have indicated, the greater its insecurity. The race is always instinctively in pursuit of perfection, always looking beyond an imperfect society, putting up with it perhaps for a long time, but in the long run invariably becoming dissatisfied with it, letting it disintegrate, and beginning anew with another.

Our American society, mainly on account of its wealth and material prosperity, has always come in for an uncommon amount of observation and criticism. Every complaint of it on the part of both native and foreign critics, as far as I am aware, is reducible to the simple thesis that it is not a civilized society. These critics do not use this precise formula, — not all of them, at least; some of them do, — but it is the sum of what they have to say, and this is as true of our most kindly critics as well as the most unkindly. It is the sum of Mrs. Trollope's observations at one end of the long array, and of Mr. Dreiser's and Mr. Sinclair Lewis's at the other. There is a complete consensus that our society leaves the claims of too many fundamental instincts unsatisfied; in fact, that we are trying to force the whole current of our being through the narrow channel set by one instinct only, the instinct of workmanship; and hence our society exhibits an extremely imperfect type of intellect and knowledge, an extremely imperfect type of religion and morals, of beauty and poetry, of social life and manners.

I am not concerned, at the moment, to comment on the soundness of this criticism; I say only that this is the sum of every criticism that has been passed on our society. Try this formula on any observer, native or foreign, and you will find, I think, that it covers the content of his opinion.

VI

Thus one is led rather seriously to wonder whether, in encouraging our women to do only the things that men can do, our feminists have not been encouraging them to take quite the wrong way with themselves. For my own part, I suspect it may be so. One may easily see how our society, if it had to, might get on without women lawyers, physicians, stockbrokers, aviators, preachers, telephone-operators, hijackers, buyers, cooks, dress-makers, bus-conductors, architects. I do not say we *should* get on without them; that is another matter entirely. I say only that we *could* get on. We *can not* get on, however, without woman as a civilizing force. We can not get on — at least, I see no way whereby we can get on — unless women apply the faculty which they have, and which men apparently have not, to the task of civilizing our society.

In encouraging women to do only what men can do, our feminists have encouraged them to put still greater stress on the instinct of workmanship, the one instinct which all critics say is already over-stressed to the breaking point; and this virtually decreases the stress on those which are already intolerably under-stressed. It causes a still more violent disturbance of balance between the claim of workmanship and the claims of intellect and knowledge, religion and morals, beauty and poetry, social life and manners. Considering the available indexes of these several claims, it would appear that our critics (I venture, after all, to give my opinion in the matter) have a good deal on their side. The development of a sense of spiritual activity as *social*, as something popular and common, in which everybody may and everyone naturally does take some sort of hand — this development seems really not to have got very far. There is, for example, a great deal of music in America; yet compare the development of our sense of music as a social expression with that which you perceive at work naturally and spontaneously in almost any German village! Similar observations may be made with regard to our literature. We all remember Mr. Duffus's examination of the state of the book-market, and we are all aware of the extremely exiguous and fear-ridden existence of anything like a serious periodical literature among us; well, compare this state of things with what one finds in France, or indeed in any Continental country, for I believe our rating is reckoned lower than any of them — as I remember, we stand eighteenth on the list of nations in this particular, though I am not sure of the exact figure; it is, at any rate, shockingly low. So one may go on, through the whole roster of spiritual activities. It appears, then, that further stress on the over-stressed instinct, and further repression on the others, are not what will do us any good.

Here, I think, comes in the point that feminism is in a position not only to direct *interest*, but, for the first time in the world's history, to direct as much purchasing-power as men have, or perhaps somewhat more. We have already seen that, in a commercial sense, women's interest controls all our organized expressions of spiritual activity. Take the advertising matter in any newspaper or magazine, and consider the proportion of it that is aimed directly at women's purchasing-power, and you can see at once how far publishing-policy must reflect specifically feminine views of life. Consider the proportion of woman's purchasing-power represented on the boards of our orchestras, in the contributions to churches, in the maintenance of schools, forums, lectureships, and you will see at once the direction that their policies must take. It is a commonplace of the theatre that the verdict of women will instantly make or break any production, instantly establish any general mode or tendency, instantly reverse one already established. Test the question of women's commercial control of organized expression anywhere in the realm of ethics, manners, art, anywhere in the realm of general culture, and your findings will be the same.

Hence it would seem that there is here a great social force out of which our society is at present getting but little good. I believe it is a much greater force than our feminism has any idea of; and this is my justification for suggesting so directly to feminism that it should recognize and measure this force, and then do everything possible to give it a better direction. Our society can not be civilized through women's attainment of the ends that feminism has hitherto set before them, laudable and excellent as those are. It can be civilized by giving an intelligent direction to the interest and the purchasing-power of women. At present these are exercised very irresponsibly and casually in the direction of civilization, largely because women have been over-preoccupied with the idea of doing what men can do. Modern feminism has unquestionably encouraged and abetted them in this preoccupation; and hence it seems competent to suggest that feminism should henceforth concern itself with recommending a higher and much more rational ideal of social usefulness.

Brussels, August, 1931
Atlantic Monthly – November, 1931

One kindly correspondent, however, sent me a very courteous letter of interest and approval, ending with the suggestion that I should write another paper . . . telling women "just what I think they ought to do" to civilize a society.

A FURTHER WORD TO WOMEN

In the preceding essay, the gist of my observations was that American women enjoy an unprecedented independence, chiefly on account of their preponderance in economic control. They own nearly half of our national wealth in their own right, and in addition to this they control a large wage-fund and a considerable allowance-fund; so that they have at present, undoubtedly, more purchasing-power than men have, and hence are pretty well able to do as they please with themselves. This being so, it occurred to me to consider what it is that they are actually doing; and appearances seemed to indicate that they mostly content themselves with doing what men do. I then ventured to suggest a field of activity which they, and especially the feminists among them, seem to have left unnoticed, and in which they would meet with no competition from men — namely, civilizing the society in which they live.

Comment on this modest proposal took a direction that interested me, and I should like to speak of it for a moment; not at all by way of complaint, for everything that came to my notice was encouraging and generous. It all pointed, however, towards what I suspect to be a very pronounced social preoccupation, and I mention it only for the sake of its evidential value, whatever this may amount to. First, then, practically all the comment on my paper was taken up with the disclosure that women own nearly half of our national wealth; it treated this fact as if it were my main point. But surely the important thing is the social implications of this fact, rather than the fact itself; and I humbly hoped that my paper had made it clear that this was the important thing. Again, all this comment seemed to assume that I was somehow chiefly concerned with the question of what women are doing with their money, whereas I was but little concerned with that; indeed, for the immediate purposes of my paper, I was not at all concerned with it.

Thus, unless I greatly misjudge it, the turn of this comment intimates a greater social preoccupation with money and the distribution of money than with the quality of human character and the direction of its development. Obviously, what a person does with his money, or with any kind of social leverage under his control, must depend finally on the sort of person he is. This being known, there is not much trouble about making a pretty accurate forecast of the general lines of use or abuse on which he will distribute his money. Hence, if one is considering people who have money, one would properly, I think, first concern oneself with the kind of people they are, rather than with the directions that their outflow of money is taking.

One kindly correspondent, however, sent me a very courteous letter of interest and approval, ending with the suggestion that I should write another paper, "a little less subtle" (her amiable euphemism for my diffidence, for subtle, alas! I could never be), telling women "just what it is I think they ought to do" to civilize a society. I suspect she guessed how tempting this large order would be to one with whom the habit of scribbling had become inveterate. If so, her guess was good, and I shall now try my best to meet it.

II

But here at the very outset a simple-minded person like myself runs into dreadful trouble over the connotation of the verb *to do*. I am afraid that even this lady's request, highly as I regard it, intimates another preoccupation characteristic of our society; I mean the characteristic preference for action rather than for thought, and especially the preference for *doing* rather than for *being* or *becoming*. Critics have remarked our inveterate persuasion that all good things will come to us of their own accord if only we keep on as hard as ever we can with doing, and let thinking go more or less by the board; and it must be said that they have a large array of evidence on their side. For example, this policy has controlled our whole economic life ever since the war; everybody has been doing, nobody has been thinking. Even now, curiously, when it is evident that this policy has not worked well, that what has been needed all along is a little less hand-over-head action and a great deal more disinterested thought, there is a general clamour for somebody to do something; thought is apparently at as great a discount as ever. Our dealings with public affairs, both economic and political, are now plainly seen to have been a series of mere improvisations; yet there is no likelihood that our policy with regard to them will change. Our society demands action, it sees public affairs only in terms of action, and action only it will have.

Hence, in the face of the two master-concerns which I have mentioned, — the concern with money and the concern with action, — a person of a direct turn of mind should be circumspect about saying what he thinks women should "do" in order to civilize a society. The first preoccupation would naturally, I think, make "doing" connote the giving of money. When men set out to "do" something for a cause, that is what it usually means; they establish trusts and foundations, and set up subsidies of one kind or another. Well, then, since our women have so much money, why not suggest that they set up a Civilization Trust somewhat on the pattern of Mr. Carnegie's Peace Trust or Mr. Rockefeller's Education Trust or Mr. Bok's International Amity Trust (I am not quite sure about these names, but the reader will at once recognize the endowments I refer to) or Mr. Eastman's Music Trust? That would be the regular thing, and very simple; all one need do is to announce the purpose, designate the trustees, and make over the money.

It would perhaps be all the simpler because women appear content to employ their money quite as men do theirs, just as they are content to employ their energy in the same occupational lines that men follow. I have pored over a great many statistics, and questioned persons who have professional knowledge of such matters, and I can find no significant difference between the sexes in this respect. Women and men alike, in a word, put most of their money into productive industry, speculate with some of it, waste a great deal of it, and some of it they give away. If, therefore, women wish to promote civilization, would they not naturally use the same means that men use, and in the same way?

The second preoccupation would almost certainly make "doing" connote some activity of an exterior and ponderable sort. In this case, I think it would probably connote something like getting up an organization, with a secretary and a constitution, a programme, perhaps some by-laws, and a "public-relations counsel" to look after publicity. Meetings would be addressed by eminent persons; papers would be read and discussed, questions asked and answered. Perhaps the organization would consider taking the matter of civilization into politics, in a tentative way; it might appoint a committee to look into the matter and report.

So why not tell my correspondent that women should first organize the idea of civilization, and then give money to promote it? That would be simple and easily understood. It would meet our society's preference for action over thought; for one may be very active in an organization and do practically no thinking at all, but, on the contrary, may let one's mind remain comfortably inaccessible and inert. It would also meet our other great preference for concerning ourselves with what a person does with his money rather than with the kind of person he is; for one may give money for a good purpose, not only without being touched by a true sentiment for that purpose, but also remaining in all respects precisely the same kind of person as before.

But the trouble about any such proposal is that civilization is an affair of the spirit, and in the realm of the spirit sheer organization and sheer money count really for very little. The preoccupations of our society being what they are, this idea is probably somewhat hard to apprehend, and hence it may bear a word or two of discussion. Organization and money are absolutely the body and blood of business and politics. They will also absolutely advance the sciences; they are a hundred per cent effective in projects like Mr. Rockefeller's institute for medical research, for example. They will also absolutely advance the arts by their scientific and mechanical side; an endowment like Mr. Eastman's gives both facilities and leisure for musically-disposed persons to improve themselves in the science and mechanics of music. But in the realm that lies beyond these, the leverage of money and organization is not direct and absolute, but indirect and relative. We are all aware, for instance, of the utter incompetence of endowments for the promotion of peace, like the Carnegie Fund and the Nobel Fund. If we were not so obsessed by the idea of an absolute universal potency of money and organization that we take it as axiomatic, we should see that peace is not to be got at in that way; it is not at all that kind of affair.

Again, education was never so highly subsidized and highly organized as in this country, and the result is so generally acknowledged to be most unsatisfactory that everybody is wondering "what to do" about it. Well, education, properly speaking, like religion, like art, like music, like international peace and amity, like any other exclusive concern of the human spirit, is fundamentally not in the money-and-organization category. Education, according to the old and sound American definition of half a century ago, is "a student sitting on one end of a log and Mark Hopkins on the other"; that is to say, it is an affair of the spirit, and as such only is it communicable; and in our devotion to our two master-preoccupations we have merely succeeded in organizing and subsidizing it pretty well off the face of the earth.

125

Not long ago a lady, dissatisfied with our general neglect of formative studies in favour of instrumental and vocational studies, resolved to "do" something to promote them; accordingly she gave an immense amount of money to one of our universities to spend in their behalf. This gift, generous as it was, obviously represents the smallest part of the undertaking; the great part lies in the management of what Prince de Bismarck used to call the imponderabilia, and one can not be as sure as one would like to be that an American university, under the heel of our two master-preoccupations, knows how to deal with these, or even knows how to discern them, or perhaps so much as knows that they exist.

So if women, like my correspondent, choose to ask what I want them to "do" in order to civilize our society, I think I should be obliged to say that I do not want them to do anything, that I mightily hope they will not try to do anything. The imponderabilia are all there is to civilization, and I know of nothing that women can "do" out of hand by way of managing them effectively. Stark organization decidedly will not answer; neither will stark money; neither, even, will interest of the conventional type. In all spiritual concerns there is something which precedes these, something which alone ever gives them the chance of being applied effectively and to good purpose. It is something a little more recondite than any of them, and far more interesting than all of them put together.

III

One of the most striking experiences of advancing age is the discovery that a great lot of formulas which our fathers foisted on us, and which we duly resented as mere disgusting cant, are true. For example, under the head of *Works before Justification*, the austere compilers of the Thirty-nine Articles declared that "for that they are not done as God willed and commanded them to be done, we doubt not but they have the nature of sin." To the ear of youth these terms sound fantastic and repulsive, yet the experience of mature years bears them out as symbolic of a profound truth. Apparently there is something in the order of nature that is against the fruition of good works done outside the purview of a rather special discipline. I do not know how to account for this; perhaps no one does; but there seems no doubt about the fact. Not only do they unaccountably fail to get the results they promised, but they somehow, against all expectation, work themselves out into actual harmfulness. Instances of this are often so impressive, even spectacular, that when the theological language of the Articles is applied to them it sounds neither forced nor archaic.

How aptly, for example, may one apply the language of purely theological formula to the whole subject of disarmament and international peace. The truth about these is, simply, that all nations would be glad to abolish war but are not willing to let go of advantages which they know they can not keep without war. Hence the indispensable condition precedent to abolishing war is that the nations should experience a change of heart and exercise repentance and seek justification by faith. It is the disinterested acceptance of a new mode of thought, and the entrance into a new spirit. Nothing else will answer; the fact is plain to anyone with any measure of common sense, and the theological language of Cranmer's day fits the fact like a plaster. Meanwhile good works like the disarmament-conferences and the Kellogg Pact are not done as God willed and commanded them to be done; that is to say, they represent no actual self-transformation on the part of the nations, nor a real desire for any. Hence they not only fail of their good intentions, but become the instruments of a peculiarly cruel deceit; they have the nature of sin.

I hope the reader will not think my Bibliolatry is excessive if I cite another incident in Christian history for the sake of developing a little further this idea of a necessary special discipline as antecedent to good works. It was never clear to me that the story told of Simon the sorcerer, in the eighth chapter of the Book of Acts, makes him out as at all a bad sort, but rather the contrary. He seems merely to have had the honest notion which we have remarked as so prevalent in our own society, that money counts for as much in the realm of the spirit as it does outside it. The Apostle's reply intimated that in Simon's case neither money nor anything else counted for much, because "his heart was not right in the sight of God," and that he had better brisk around and transform himself into the sort of creature who could see things differently; and Simon appears to have taken the suggestion in good part, as giving him an entirely new idea and one worth thinking about.

All this leads directly to a clear and positive view of woman's relation to the task of civilizing our society. What she "does" in this relation is not, logically, the first thing to be considered; the first thing is what she does with herself. In their due season it would be very profitable and interesting to discuss money and organization and many other possible modes of an exterior and ponderable "doing," but their season is as yet remote. *Porro unum est necessarium* — the thing now is to discuss terms of a valid conversion, a change of heart, and entrance into a new life and a new spirit, under the generative power of a new and high ideal. I am aware that this pulpiteering phraseology courts offense, but I use it deliberately because the two master-preoccupations of our society are so strong that one's only chance to make any headway against them is by the force of language that is downright enough to startle their votaries out of an instinctive mechanical obedience. Having done so, I may now clear myself from any imputation of priggishness by saying in all good faith that I am not urging a moral duty on our women. My mind is furthest from that; I am merely suggesting an interesting opportunity. Nor am I appealing to any altruistic motive, — none whatever, — but to one of an entirely different order, which I shall speak of just as soon as I have made my main point a little clearer.

IV

The steady approach to social, political and industrial equality of the sexes, and the steady shift of sanctions, conventions and moralities concerning all the sex-relationships therein implied, have brought out a spiritual phenomenon which, from the point of view of civilization, is disturbing. Women at large accommodate themselves not only to doing what men do, but also to accepting the general standard of values that men have set. They take their views of life as a hand-me-down from men, and model their demands on life by those of men. Observation of women in active life, in politics, business, the professions, leaves no room for doubt of this; and it is as clearly observable, often more so, in leisure-class women. They accept the motivation which men have given our society; they fall in with it and make it their own.

It must be understood that I am not complaining of this, for they are bred to these spiritual acceptances; all the social pressure that is brought to bear upon them, from the cradle up, tends that way. The fact and its consequences remain, however, and are to be remarked without prejudice. Only the other day, one of our most thoughtful and serious writers spoke of our country as "so hard ridden and so little blessed" by its womanhood. The observation is not new; and it is true because the social realignment of the sexes has brought woman's views of life, her demands on life, her ideals of society, her aspirations, the practical direction of her intuitions, into an increasingly close agreement with those of men.

Here, then, is the condition that impairs and enervates the faculty which women have, and which men apparently have not, for civilizing a society. It is an *inward* condition; that is the point I would dwell on. It is relatively nothing serious that women should acquiesce in various formal and external adaptations to a society which men have motivated, — a society, let us say, which proposes statistics as a reasonable and satisfying substitute for philosophy, religion and romance, — but it is very serious indeed that they should acquiesce in an *inward* adaptation to it. There is no great harm done by women's sharing with men all the material comforts, assistances and gratifications available in a rich and powerful society; but there is great harm in their sharing men's inward persuasion that these are all that a properly constituted society may be asked to provide. That women join with men in giving play to the instinct of expansion is all well enough; that instinct is part of their being. But the case is far different where they join with men in a view of this instinct as the only one whose expression is to be taken seriously; and in a corresponding belief that an expression of the race's other fundamental social instincts — the instincts of intellect and knowledge, of religion and morals, of beauty and poetry, of social life and manners — is to be regarded casually and irresponsibly, as something outside the serious business of life, and in which one's participation is to be determined by fashion or by fancy.

Until this disability, which, as I have said, is now forced upon women by all kinds of social pressure — until this is removed, not much can be effectively "done" toward civilizing a society.

In my judgment this disability, resulting as it does in a decay of faculty, is the most calamitous that women have ever suffered. In my former paper I called our feminists' attention to this, though in my diffidence I did it rather playfully; still, I hoped they might penetrate to my suggestion and take it in good part. I am myself, I hope, too good a feminist not to be appalled by the monstrous price that women are paying for such advantages as their approach to legal, social and industrial equality has brought them; that price being the weakening of an invaluable special faculty — let me say, the surrender of an *ad hoc* superiority — through their broad general assumption of "the male psychology" toward their newer interests and toward life at large. Though my love for equality and justice approaches fanaticism, I can yet understand how, with this price levied against it, woman's progress in emancipation might be thought to have come a trifle high.

Thus the upshot of my theological language of a moment ago is that in order effectively to "do" anything for civilization the individual woman must revive this moribund faculty and get it into a convalescent state by a deliberate revision of her views of life and her demands on life. It is a task for the individual only, a straight job of self-transformation; and the freer one is to do it, the easier, naturally, it will be.

This was all I had in mind when in my former paper I brought up the point that our women have so much money. The possession of it rids them of the most powerful of all social pressures — economic pressure — to shape their spiritual nature by man's pattern. Certainly not all our women have this freedom, certainly nothing like a majority have it; but, as I intimated in my half-jocose little allegory of the fashion in clothes, if those only who have it would make it serve them in this task of self-transformation, we should have a new world.

V

This task implies, in general terms, first, that woman should get as complete an understanding of the claims of the four neglected social instincts, and as acute and lively a sense of their validity, as she has shown herself able to get of the claims of the instinct of expansion. The lady buyer, broker, executive, politician, knows precisely what these latter claims are; she is as perspicacious about them as any male colleague; you can not fool her about them for a moment. She also has no doubt whatever about their validity. They are abundantly real to her; her assumption of "the male psychology" toward them has in fact made their reality mount up to an enormous preponderance, as practically the ultimate reality to which her being responds. Women, then, especially those who are free of economic hindrance, may carry just these powers of perspicacity, concentration and assurance over into the realm of the spirit, and employ them in just this way for bringing their inner nature into a larger conformity with the best that one finds there.

That is what the notable women of the French and Italian Renaissance did. In looking over their record with this clue in mind, I was interested to see how intelligently and perseveringly they made a business of spiritual activity; as real a business as our emancipated sisters now make of promoting bond-issues, practising law or hawking cosmetics. The realm of the spirit was as real to them, as engaging to their powers, as the realm of politics; and the discipline necessary to make them at home in it — "the intending of the mind," to borrow Newton's phrase — was as familiar and as cogently practical to them as the discipline of arithmetic.

The task of self-transformation implies, further, a great engagement of the emotions; just such an engagement as that which now invigorates and fortifies woman in meeting so competently the claims of the instinct of expansion. She now throws an immense deal of sound affection, honourable pride, even a great deal of pseudo-romantic vision, into her stock-jobbing or cosmetic-peddling; the natural forces which she confronts in the course of these pursuits are such as foster them and call them into play. The psychology of "pepping up sales" is in a sense sound; it contemplates the focusing of just these emotions by clearing and stimulating a sense of these natural forces as a challenge. Perhaps the most impressive example of its effectiveness in the service of the instinct of expansion is seen in the concentration of Russia's emotional power upon the Five-Year Plan. Well, the women of the Renaissance, while remaining in all respects women of the world, not only disciplined their intellect, but also disciplined and stimulated their emotions into just such a profound concentration upon the natural forces which they found confronting them in the realm of the spirit. They dealt with the great natural forces of mystery, the forces of beauty, the forces of love, as ably and as passionately as our well-disciplined modern woman deals with the forces of supply and demand.

Thus these women were great civilizers, probably without knowing it, and certainly with no self-conscious effort. They seem not to have laboured under the sense of a special mission to society; what they "did" appears to have been largely occasional. But they were nobly serious with themselves, their eye was single; and their record makes one sometimes suspect that civilization is perhaps — just possibly — best promoted by indirection. One especially suspects this when one observes the very puny results accruing from direct, self-conscious efforts to promote it. But, however this may be, one may believe that, if the personality of our women reflected a spiritual discipline at all commensurate with the freedom that their economic independence allows for its undertaking, there would be no need to worry much about any secondary means of enhancing that personality's effectiveness upon society. Its contagion would find its own ways, and perhaps all the more easily without conscious guidance.

One can not be more specific than this without the risk of presumption; how should I particularize to women upon the incidence of a special faculty which they have and I have not? If I should offer the detailed "constructive suggestions" that are always in popular demand, and any confiding woman undertook to follow them, she would no doubt make a great mess of it, and I should merely become one more example, among many in my sex, of the futility of trying to show one's grandmother how to sift ashes. Taking my stand firmly on the side of reason and prudence, I shall confine myself to clearing away a possible slight suspicion of inconsistency.

VI

It may be asked, if I doubt that civilization is much furthered by direct self-conscious endeavour, why I should write an article intimating that something of the kind is called for. If women are not to transform themselves in obedience to a social motive, why should they do it at all? Well, the social motive is very noble and elevated; I have all possible reverence for it; yet I am reluctant to recommend it, feeling, like the Psalmist, that I should not be meddling in great matters which are too high for me. I prefer to leave this sort of exhortation to the sociologists and political liberals, who are handier at it than I am, and content myself with suggesting a motive that is less grandiose but quite as valid, and, if possible, perhaps a shade more congenial.

When someone asked the physicist Michelson why he worked so hard over measuring the speed of light, he replied that he did it because it was such great fun. That is the only motive that I would suggest — happiness. Apparently the women of the Renaissance had no other; quite unconscious of any exalted social mission, they seem to have worked like beavers at remaking themselves merely for the enjoyment they got out of doing it. Probably, indeed, there is no happiness like this, once the initial obstacles are got over. Even the cold and profound thought of Bishop Butler takes on a faint glow of warmth in contemplating it, for he says that, if it were not for the practical difficulties attending the process, the enjoyment of self-transformation would hardly be distinguishable from a kind of sensuality. But one need say no more on this subject; it is one on which the humblest intellects are in agreement with the philosophers and saints, for it is open to the supreme test which anyone is able to apply — the test of experience.

Happiness; only that. At the present time it is uncommonly clear that our overindulgence of the instinct of expansion has got us into a most unhappy pickle. Political and economic imperialism; a great war; desperate collisions of interest in the consolidation of gains; the reign of a purblind and truculent nationalism; a lunatic contempt of immutable economic laws; a period of unexampled collapse, prostration, anxiety, and wretchedness; well, there we are! For some of us — I hope many — the worst of our tangle will begin to unwind, I think soon; but the question is, What then?

Should it not presently occur to independent women, even to some of those who have gone furthest with "the male psychology," that the instinct of expansion has been a trifle overworked, and that perhaps the male psychology towards it was not an unqualified good thing for women to assume? Would it not strike them as worth while now to make a stringent revision of their whole standard of values, to ease off some of the stress on the claims of expansion and bring those of the other fundamental instincts into some kind of balance and harmony with them? I do not put these questions in a general way. I ask only whether it might not occur to these women that they would themselves be happier if something of the sort should take place *within them*. Over and above the immediate issues of the day, the present period seems to me to force the question whether a life made up, on its serious side, of an exclusive concern with the claims of expansion, and, on its lighter side, of an exclusive concern with the *curiosités qui ne peuvent nous donner qu'une sensation egoïste et passagère* — whether this life can be permanently interesting; interesting, I mean, primarily to those who are able to control its quality. Does such a life offer enough happiness to make it worth living, even to those who dominate and shape it?

"One is inclined," as Stendhal said of us, years ago, "to say that the source of sensibility is dried up in this people. They are just, they are reasonable, but they are essentially not happy." When a journalist asked Mr. Edison on his last birthday, I think, or next to the last, what he thought about human happiness, he replied simply, "I am not acquainted with anyone who is happy." There is no need of documentary testimony on this point; the faces that one sees and the voices that one hears are enough to establish it. May I say also, as discreetly as possible, that even the faces and voices of our economically independent women are not those of happy people? Why should they be; how *can* they be? Our whole national history may be fairly epitomized as a ruthless rampage of the instinct of expansion upon a vast field of exploitable rich-ness; and, with the claims of the other social instincts thus con-tinuously sacrificed to the claims of expansion for a century and a half, how can even the beneficiaries of this rampage be happy?

The thing is impossible, for, as we all know, every unused or misused or misinterpreted instinct becomes a source of uneasiness.

I suspect that even men are now somewhat reluctantly suggestible about the quality of the collective life which they have created; there are some signs that this is a season of repentance. Perhaps even we, some of us, — I speak as a man, — are beginning to think that things might go better if all hands were a little happier; if there were a little less recourse to raw sensation in the quest of happiness, and a more resolute clearing of the inner springs of joy. Possibly we might incline more favourably than heretofore toward the idea of a life that gives a little less play to the instinct that we have so horribly over-driven, and a little more to those that we have repressed and deformed; a collective life, in short, that does not flatly preclude the enjoyment of a humane and reasonable happiness. But although we may regard the idea of such a life rather thoughtfully, just now perhaps even wistfully, we have no faculty for realizing it. Women have; and if the women who are economically free would abandon "the male psychology," and so remodel their inner nature as merely to liberate this faculty, they would need give no thought to what they should "do" in order to apply it socially. It would apply itself.

Brussels, November, 1931
Atlantic Monthly – March, 1932

"*for life to be fruitful, life must be felt as a joy; that it is by the bonds of joy, not of happiness or pleasure, not of duty or responsibility, that the called and chosen spirits are kept together in this world.*"

— George Sand as quoted by AJN in his introduction to
  The Selected Works of Artemus Ward

FOUNTAINS OF JOY

Current discussions of the philosophy of art remind us that, according to Goethe, a little common sense will sometimes do duty for a great deal of philosophy, but no amount of philosophy will make up for a failure in common sense. It is usually the case that as analysis becomes closer and philosophizing becomes more profound, there is a tendency to obscure certain broad general fundamentals which to the eye of common sense are always apparent; and thus very often the complete truth of the matter is imperfectly apprehended. A great deal of what we read about the arts seems in some such fashion as this to get clear away from the notion that the final purpose of the arts is to give joy; yet common sense, proceeding in its simple, unmethodical manner, would say at once that this is their final purpose, and that one who did not keep it in mind as such, could hardly hope to arrive at the truth about any of the arts. Matthew Arnold once said most admirably that no one could get at the actual truth about the Bible, who did not enjoy the Bible; and that one who had all sorts of fantastic notions about the origin and composition of the Bible, but who knew how to enjoy the Bible deeply, was nearer the truth about the Bible than one who could pick it all to pieces, but could not enjoy it. Common sense, we believe, would hold this to be true of any work of art.

When Hesiod defined the function of poetry as that of giving "a release from sorrows and a truce from cares," he intimated the final purpose of all great art as that of elevating and sustaining the human spirit through the communication of joy, of felicity;

that is to say, of the most simple, powerful and highly refined emotion that the human spirit is capable of experiencing. This, no doubt, does not exhaust its beneficence; no doubt it works for good in other ways as well; but this is its great and final purpose. It is not to give entertainment or diversion or pleasure, not even to give happiness, but to give joy; and through this distinction, common sense comes immediately upon a test of good and valid art, not infallible, perhaps, but nevertheless quite competent. It is, in fact, the test that the common sense of mankind always does apply, consciously or unconsciously, to determine the quality of good art. Great critics, too, from Aristotle down, have placed large dependence on it. One wonders, therefore, whether more might not advantageously be made of it in the critical writing of the present time.

A work of art — a poem or novel, a picture, a piece of music — may affect the average cultivated spirit with interest, with curiosity, with pleasure; it may yield diversion, entertainment or even solace, not in the sense of edification or tending to build up a permanent resource against sorrows and cares, but in the sense that its pleasurable occupation of the mind excludes sorrow and care for the time being, somewhat as physical exercise or a game of chess or billiards may do. But all this is not a mark of good art. Good art affects one with an emotion of a different quality; and this quality may be rather easily identified, provided one does not make a great point of proceeding with the stringency of a philosopher in trying to define it. Joubert said that it is not hard to know God, if one will only not trouble oneself about defining him; and this is true as well of the profound and obscure affections of the human spirit — they are much better made know in the experience of the devout than in the analysis of the philosopher. A critic, indeed, might content himself at the outset by laying down some examples of classic art, and saying that the emotion he wishes to identify, the emotion of joy, is simply what is produced upon the average cultivated spirit by *those*; and that the difference in quality between this emotion and the emotion produced by another work of art, is a fair index or registration of the difference in quality of art between the two objects or examples. We have space but for one illustration, so for convenience we shall take it from the realm of poetry. Let us take two examples, both dealing with the valid and excellent poetic theme of the shortness of human life and the transitory character of its interests. First, this one:

> How nothing must we seem unto this ancient thing!
> How nothing unto the earth — and we so small!
> O, wake, wake! do you not feel my hands cling?
> One day it will be raining as it rains to-night; the same wind blow,
> Raining and blowing on this house wherein we lie, but you and I,
> We shall not hear, we shall not ever know.

Is the emotion wherewith this verse affects the average cultivated spirit, of the same order, the same quality, as the emotion produced by this —

> The cloud-cap'd towers, the gorgeous palaces,
> The solemn temples, the great globe itself,
> Yea, all which it inherit, shall dissolve
> And, like an insubstantial pageant faded,
> Leave not a rack behind. We are such stuff
> As dreams are made on, and our little life
> Is rounded with a sleep.

— or is the difference merely one of degree? Well, then this difference may be used at the outset by criticism, as the common sense of mankind does continually use it, as an index of the poetic quality of the two examples; and criticism can go safely on in assuming that to whatever degree a work of art succeeds in arousing just *that* emotion, so far can it justify its candidacy for a place as valid art.

We do not put forward this test as one to be used mechanically, nor have we any exaggerated notion of its importance. There are some very welcome signs that criticism, after long running derelict in fantastic extravagance, is beginning to come to its sober senses. Well, then, here, in this test that we speak of, is an implement of criticism that great critics have found extremely useful, but which has of late fallen into disuse — why not bring it out and use it again, not fanatically, but with judgment and discretion? It is primarily an implement for the critic to use upon himself in shaping the course of his criticism; the layman, as we said, has had the more or less conscious use of it all the time. When confronted with the claims of this or that work of art, the critic will be greatly helped to get his bearings if for the moment he puts all other considerations aside, and asks himself with what order or quality of emotion, precisely, does this work of art affect *him*. Is it with a pleasurable emotion due to interest, curiosity, entertainment, diversion, or is it the emotion of felicity, of joy? No matter about the degree, but is it or is it not, in any measure, small or great, the *kind* of thing that he gets out of "The cloud-cap'd towers, the gorgeous palaces"? We do not say that this test will ensure his judgment; all we say is that it will greatly assist it.

Freeman – March, 1923

I take it that an interesting person in literature is just what he is in life. He is the kind of person who powerfully stirs your fancy and imagination, so that you want to go back to him and see him again and again, and keep on seeing him as much as you can.

On Making Low People Interesting

Having lived of late in a part of Europe where there is very little doing in the way of English, I went for many months without reading a word in my own tongue. By working in a different set of sequences so long, my mind got a bit away from the familiar ones; it rather slacked off on the English-reading habit, as I suppose any mind that has any flexibility is bound to do. But not thinking about this, I was not conscious of the change while it was going on, and when at the end of a long period I fell heir to a dozen cast-off English novels I was surprised to find that I approached them a good deal like a stranger. On this account, I suppose, certain features of them seemed more odd and unusual than they would have seemed if I had not so completely broken with the English-reading habit, and broken also so largely with the life which they represented.

Some of these novels were British, some American, and all were recent, several being of the current crop, and none more than a couple of years old, I think. They were all good sellers, and had been much talked about. One feature common to them all was that they dealt with low people. I cannot recall a single character out of the whole lot whom one would not rate as pretty distinctly low. This was all to the good, for low people are a great asset to an artist. He can do more with them than with any other kind, because their lives give him a larger range, being lived in a freer fashion, less subject to external directions and restraints. But what impressed me most was that not one of these low people was interesting. Not one of them had anything which touched off the waiting fancy and imagination of the reader. I take it that an interesting person in literature is just what he is in life. He is the kind of person who powerfully stirs your fancy and imagination, so that you want to go back to him and see him again and again, and keep on seeing him as much as you can. None of these people was like that. Bring one of them to life, and you would not cross the street to meet him or give a button to get acquainted with him. They were all so colourless in fact, so unsubstantial for literary purposes, that the authors had to be continually helping them out, finding something lively for them to do, creating one striking situation after another, to keep them going. This threw over the story a general air of fictitiousness and unreality which was dissatisfying. One novel, for instance, which dealt with the progress of a hard-fisted, bull-headed English farmer-girl on her way to prosperity, culminated in her acquisition of an illegitimate child. This episode had a touch of embarrassment about it, as of something which did not belong there but had been lugged in by the ears. One might say at first sight that it was put in at a publisher's suggestion, as a gratuitous handful of incense to what Matthew Arnold called "the great goddess Aselgeia." Still, as one thought it over, there was little else for the poor girl to do, little else that was within her competence. If she had been an interesting character she need not have done it. Some one once asked Thackeray whether Becky Sharp actually did or did not "go wrong," and Thackeray replied that, for the life of him, he didn't know.

The only interest that I could discover in these stories, therefore, was in virtue of various literary devices, some legitimate, ingenious, and workman-like, and others rather ramshackle. There was not a vestige of character-portrayal that was anywhere near above par; no vestige of the art that creates a character interesting in itself, irrespective of plot and dramatic action, powerfully stimulating the reader's fancy and imagination, like the forty Flemish types in Old Breughel's sketch-book — just faces, studies in feature and expression, nothing more — but what faces! Still, as

I said, I had been long away from my native life and letters, and did not feel sure of my judgment; so I rummaged around for something to true up by, and finally emerged with a copy of the *Pickwick Papers*.

There are eighty-two characters in that book, not counting those in the inserted stories, which come to sixteen more, I think; say about a hundred, all told. Regarded as folks, nearly all of them are low; and those whom one might not class precisely as low are middling ordinary. Even the virtues of Pickwick himself are prosaic. None of these people would ever set the river afire with his genius or make one's head swim with the elevation of his spirit. The great majority, I think, would be put down at once as the very riddlings of creation. But how *interesting!* — why, one would walk miles unending to meet one of them and, having met him, would haunt him, and delightedly follow him up and down the earth. Not especially the major characters, either, but those who appear and disappear in the course of half a page, whose personalities are so clearly and vividly struck out in a single paragraph that the reader's fancy and imagination instantly get their whole measure for life by a kind of flashlight photography. Think of Mr. Smangle, Pott, Mr. Peter Magnus, Grummer, Pell, Dowler, Mr. Leo Hunter, Bantam; think of Bob Sawyer, and of his landlady, Mrs. Raddle! It is conceded that Dickens did little with female character and did not seem interested in it, and this has led some critics to say that he was not able to do much with it. I suggest that this assumption runs hard aground on Mrs. Raddle. But there those people are, low as they can be, mostly the sheer scum of the earth, none of them really doing anything in particular — the book has hardly any literary machinery even at the outset, and promptly drops what little it starts with. There they are — that is practically all one can say about them, and since they are what they are, it is all one need say.

The *Pickwick Papers*, however, are rather a special kind of literary product. The preface tells us that they are not meant to be the conventional type of novel, but a loosely organized aggregation of individual characters run together on a weak thread of commonplace adventure. So, as well as I could without having the book at hand, I revived my recollections of Dickens's next story, which is in all respects quite the regular thing. *Nicholas Nickleby* has a formal plot, well worked out in plenty of dramatic action, for whatever these devices amount to; other authors have done as well with both, and some better. There, again, it is character, mostly of the very lowest, that gives this book its hold upon the reader's fancy and imagination. Mantalini, Gride, Crummles and his barnstormers, the Kenwigses, Squeers, Noggs, Lillyvick — surely the rarest assortment of utter riff-raff, of sheer human sculch, that was ever raked together between two covers, but *interesting* beyond expression. The plot of *Nicholas Nickleby* might be what it liked, the dramatic action might go this way or that way, and no one would give a penny for the difference. So long as these people are what they are, who cares what they do? Let them stand out and mark time, if they choose, like the characters in *Pickwick*, for all the odds it would make. Imagine some go-getting publisher telling Charles Dickens that to "sustain the human interest," and really to "put the book over with a bang," he ought to get Kate Nickleby in the family way by Sir Mulberry Hawk, and fork in all the biological details of the episode that the law allows!

II

But Dickens is Dickens, and one may not expect the average run of authorship to match him, and certainly one would not wish it to imitate him. One might reasonably expect it to emulate him, however, if indeed character-portrayal be any longer regarded as part of authorship's job. The samples I had been assaying did not show traces of any such effort, so I resolved to look farther into the matter. When I came back into the English-speaking world, therefore, I began to persecute my whole literary acquaintance for points on the status of character-portrayal. Was it by way of becoming a lost art, and if so, why? There seemed to be a complete consensus of opinion that it was. Cultivated amateurs and those whose connection with literature is professional told me that character in current English fiction was becoming standardized into a very few types, and that even those few were vague and vapid. As for my second question, I got various answers which I think may be susceptible of synthesis.

To begin with a rather extreme view, a brisk young acquaintance of mine, who is fond of drawing distinctions in favour of "this generation" and "the modern spirit in art" (probably noticing that I am getting on in years and my critical guns a little honeycombed) tells me that no one cares any more for character-portrayal. This shift in taste is due to "the new psychology" — whatever that is — and the thing nowadays is to produce a kind of literary chart or graph of "what goes on in a person's mind." The acme of achievement in the new art is reached, I believe, when one succeeds in showing by what seems a pretty strictly journalistic method "how he got that way." I speak cautiously about these matters, for I feel uncertain about them, not sure that I understand them very well. Like Artemus Ward, I skurcely kno what those air. As well as I can judge, however, one of the novels in my original exhibit would seem to come somewhere near filling my young friend's bill.

It was rather literally the inside story of the development, if one may call it that, of a young girl of the period, a flapper. This flapper was a filthy little trollop — which I hasten to say is no objection to her, for many great characters in fiction are shocking trollops. A trollop is a first-rate literary property, plenty good enough for anybody as far as she goes; but *qua* trollop, she does not go very far, and a good artist knows it. His literary instinct warns him that in this capacity alone she is worth only about a stickful, nonpareil, on the eighth page, last column. If he wants her to be a real headliner, he must freight her up with something more substantial for literary purposes.

But this young woman was a trollop all the time, twenty-four hours a day, being apparently devoid of any other faculty. She was

149

good for nothing else. This gave the story a pathological turn — a turn of very special and extremely limited interest, quite ludicrously inadequate to the amount of space employed to tell it. I was reminded by contrast, though the stories have essentially something in common, of Bill Nye's story of an omnivorous dog that he once had, named Entomologist, who ate some liquid plaster-of-Paris one day, and did not survive the experiment. Bill held an autopsy and salvaged the plaster for a memento, using it as a paperweight, with the inscription, "Plaster cast of Entomologist, taken by himself — interior view." This was as much of a story as these humble literary properties were worth, and Bill was enough of a literary artist to refrain from trying to stretch it. Consequently, as far as he goes, Entomologist is an interesting figure; he stirs one's fancy and imagination in a small way, but an agreeable way, and sets them at work reconstructing the circumstances and filling in the details for oneself. A good artist is one who prods up one's fancy and imagination to do all this sort of work. If the creator of this flapper had been anything of an artist, her annals would have amounted to a paragraph. I think I know what went on in Mr. Jingle's mind most of the time, quite as well as if Dickens had psychologized and analyzed him and delivered long-winded disquisitions on how he got that way.

This may be the logical place to comment on one general tendency common to the dozen novels that formed my *corpus vile* for dissection. They all dealt largely with sex-relations, usually irregular. Complaint of this tendency is common enough, but the ground of complaint never seemed to me well taken, and I always wondered why so much should be made of bad reasons for complaining of it when it is just as easy to propose a good one. Sexual irregularities are in themselves unobjectionable for literary purposes, as far as I can see, and I think it is simply silly to pretend a "moral issue" in their treatment. The real trouble is with the author's own relation to his subject. An author's own obvious preoccupation with sexual affairs, regular or irregular — I say obvious, because one can discern it instantly — is objectionable, for the reason that the amount of actual literary material which these affairs provide is never enough to satisfy this preoccupation. It will not go far in the construction of a novel; and his preoccupation keeps him trying to make it go farther than it will go.

For instance, one of the novels in my exhibit propounded a curious prairie-dog's nest of unwholesome mortals, whose whole existence seemed to be made up of pigging together in joyous squalor through three hundred solid pages. This was the total impression conveyed by the story, and it was most unpleasantly dull. Not a character in the book had the slightest pretension to interest — one listlessly wished they would all go off together down a steep place into the sea and get drowned, like their lineal forefathers of Gadara. A very good story can be made of the antecedents and consequences of any mode or form of concubinage, from marriage up and down, but the actual technique of concubinage itself is not diversified enough to permit a writer to do anything with it worth speaking of. It is too undifferentiated, except for subjective conditions which are not reproducible upon a reader. Except for these conditions, which are potent enough but quite unreproducible upon a third person, living with one woman is almost precisely like living with another — even the standard jokes and cartoons on the subject show that; and if it be so in life which brings into play all the small interest-provoking accidents of social contact and entourage, the general effect of which also is quite unreproducible, how much more so in literature!

To make the case clearer, let us introduce a couple of parallels from one, by the way, who is the unquestioned master in the art of showing "what goes on in a person's mind" — from Tourgueniev. *First Love*, to begin with, is a story of low people; only one person in it, the narrator, is anything but a very poor affair. The heroine, Zinaïda, is a flapper of seventeen or so. Here you have the real thing in flappers and the real thing in trollops. *Qua* flapper and *qua* trollop, Zinaïda makes the candidates put forward by our

151

contemporary literature look like Confederate money. The bare
story is squalid and repulsive; a journalistic report of it would be
unreadable. But as Tourgueniev unfolds it, the great goddess Lu-
bricity gets not a single grain of incense. Not one detail is propounded for the satisfaction of prurience. The people, dreadful as
they are, and the drama, weighted as it is with all that is unnatural and shocking in Zinaïda and her paramour, are more than
interesting; they are profoundly moving, they release a flow of
sympathy that effaces all other emotions, and one lays down the
book with a sense of being really humanized and bettered by
having read it. Let the reader get it in Mrs. Garnett's excellent
translation, and experiment for himsel. Then let him go even
farther, and try *Torrents of Spring*. This is a story of the antecedents and consequences of adultery plus seduction, brought about
under inconceivably loathsome circumstances. The three princi-
pal characters are detestably low. The foremost among them, Maria
Nikolaevna, in my judgment the most interesting woman in the
whole range of fiction — what would one not give to see her and
talk with her for an hour? — is the world's prize slut, if ever there
were one. But the author has not the slightest preoccupation
with her sluttishness, and hence he communicates none to the
reader, and the great goddess Aselgeia goes begging again.

III

Some of my literary acquaintances whom I have questioned
tell me that authors write too fast. Eager to satisfy the market,
they do not take time to portray character. I doubt the force of
this. Dickens wrote furiously against time all his life. Haste drove
him into some pretty indifferent grammar sometimes, and often
loosened his constructions. But it never switched him off from a
straight drive at the essential features of character. If he sketched
an individual in seven strokes, you "get" that individual — you
get him all. Those seven are the essential strokes, and you can fill
in the rest for yourself without any trouble. In this power of

instant penetration to the essential he is like Old Breughel. Haste should not interfere with this power in the modern artist, if he has it. It might make him a little slovenly in his technical expression of the essentials after he has caught them, but it should not impair his ability to catch them. It seems to me, therefore, that this explanation will not wash.

Another said that authorship nowadays did not compose with its eye on the object. Its vision wavered about sometimes on the object, sometimes on arbitrary formulas of interpretation set by publishing-policy, sometimes on possible liberties to be taken with the reader's mind, and so on. But if an artist's eye wanders, he is aware of it; he tears up his sketch, curses himself once or twice, and starts all over again. He knows at once where the trouble is. If he did not he would be no artist, and should be advised to give up literature and take to something else. This criticism, therefore, amounts to saying that we have no artists, or the chance of any, which I doubt. I doubt it on the strength of collateral evidence presented by some of the novels that I am discussing. Another said that current authorship did not know enough about human beings; its experience was superficial and journalistic, not going deep enough to provide a mature, objective, but kindly insight. There is no doubt something in this, but if so, I suggest that it only moves the problem one step backward. Granted that the author has not enough depth of experience, why does not the instinct of an artist make him bestir himself and get it?

My notion is that the author is not altogether at fault. It takes more than the man to make an artist; it takes the combination of the man and the moment, the man and the *milieu*. An artist must have models, and for him to have them, the civilization around him must produce them. Old Breughel sketched marvellously interesting faces, but the faces were there for him to sketch; the civilization of Brussels produced them, as it still does — you can see a hundred an hour there, any day. British literature, up to a half-century ago, has been peculiarly rich in interesting character — well, British life was peculiarly rich in it. By all accounts, London of 1827 was swarming with models for Dickens.

No doubt the modern author might do better than he does, since we all might well do that, but I suggest that he cannot be expected to do inordinately better than the civilization around him provides him the technical means of doing. A physician once told me that smallpox had been so far subdued that a whole generation of physicians had come on who had never seen a case; and if one of them by chance did encounter a stray case, he had nothing but booklearning to meet it with. If an author does not reproduce a character of interesting distinction, it is fair to ask how many such characters he ever saw. If his insight into character is superficial, it is fair to ask how much opportunity his civilization ever gave him for deepening it. If his people — especially his low people, his flappers and trollops, his ragamuffins and adventurers — lack savour and individuality, how many such people has he ever known who actually had more? If his types are few and standardized, how about his practicable models? It is rather significant, I think, that the best work, the most artistic work, in character-portrayal done in America is done upon models furnished by encysted cultures, by people who cleave with obstinate tenacity to their traditional bent, and maintain it against the levelling force of the civilization around them — the Irish, for example, and the Jews. Even so capable and experienced a writer as Willa Cather never succeeded in depicting character as she has done in her last book by going back to a transplanted civilization for available models. Potash and Perlmutter, their bloodthirsty competitors, their operators and finishers, their wives' relations, are all really pretty dreadful people, but what profoundly interesting characters they are, how vivid, brilliant, and individual are their qualities! In actual life, too, they are pretty dreadful people. I sometimes think there will be a record-breaking pogrom in New York some day, and there are occasions even now when the most peace-loving person among us wishes he could send over for a couple of *sotnias* of Cossacks to floor-manage the subway rush. But if one can get on an isle of safety somewhere and survey them, how absorbingly *interesting* they are. Think of Mr. Goldblatt and his son-in-law, of Henry Feigenbaum and, above all of Uncle Mosha Kronberg! — there is an interesting individual for you, as full of fascinations as a cucumber is of seeds.

I once asked an American portrait-painter, a very good one, how many faces had ever turned up in the day's work that really challenged his artistic insight and penetration, like the innumerable great faces put on the canvas by Maes, Hals, Steen, Rembrandt, Fabritius, Koninck, de Backer, and a host of others. He said perhaps two or three. I know that on my return to America after a long soj ourn among Belgian types, the most striking impression made upon me was of the curiously uniform, undistinguished, characterless quality of the faces about me. There were perhaps half a hundred Americans on the ship with me, and for two days after we landed, while I was getting my sea-legs off and becoming used to my surroundings, I kept seeing those people all over New York. It was an extremely odd experience. Of course it was not the same person in any case, but each one of the whole series of resemblances was strong enough to take me in for several minutes. What can a portrait painter do? Similarly, what can a literary artist do?

Moreover, the freemasonry of *was uns alle bändigt, das Gemeine* affects the reading public, as well as the artist, in an unfavorable way. No one can make much out of Dickens without some knowledge of the economic and social life of his day. The appreciation of his power of character-portrayal is largely a matter of the interest bred by general information and general culture. When I saw the play "Potash and Perlmutter" some years ago, I seemed to be the only person in the house who was not a Jew. I saw it twice more, and remarked the same phenomenon. I wondered how its power of character-portrayal, much better felt in the stories than in the play, of course, affected the average of the *Goyim*; whether their general level of culture was high enough to enable them disinterestedly to appraise it for what it was worth. Several times, at a period when I was in a position to do so, I have experimented with promising young sprigs of the hire learning, who had "specialized in English literature," *Gott soll hüten*, by noting what signs they showed of sparking up over great examples of character-portrayal. I never got my investment back. If I got a net of three cents on the dollar I was as elated as if I had found it in the street. Since those days, when I have see my countrymen pausing before portraits done by the old Flemish masters, I have wondered what impression was made upon them by the faces themselves, as indices of character.

IV

I, therefore, suggest, with all possible delicacy, that hopes of "the great American novel" are extravagant. This art requires great subjects; and the life about us does not provide them. It requires a very special order of correspondence between the artist and his environment; and the life about us does not promote this or even permit it. Our civilization, rich and varied as it may be, is not *interesting*; its general level falls too far below the standard set by the collective experience of mankind. If one points with pride to our endless multiplication of the mechanics of existence, and our incessant unintelligent preoccupation with them, the artist replies that with all this he can do nothing. What he demands is great and interesting character, character that powerfully stirs the fancy and imagination, and a civilization in which such interests are dominant cannot supply it.

Today's newspapers carry an item from one of our mid-Western towns, saying that in a raid on some swindling charlatan the police discovered hundreds of letters from people who were burdened with intolerable tedium, which they declared they would do anything in the world to escape "if only he would advise them how." Yet these people had an available apparatus of comfort and of enjoyment surpassing anything ever seen in the world. No doubt they had movies handy, and money enough to patronize them, since the submerged tenth does not write to frauds. Probably many of them had Ford cars, and radio sets yielding jazz to dance by; probably they were better dressed and fed, and more comfortably housed, than people of a station corresponding to theirs have ever been! But all this did not make for an interesting life; and they knew so little what such a life consisted in, and the terms on which it was to be had, that they turned to this wretched fellow's nostrum, whatever it was, in pathetic and ignorant hope. Their case is common; everyone knows that it is, let him pretend as he chooses. Everyone is aware that the failure of our civilization is precisely this failure in *interest*, for which nothing can make up. Our collective life is not "lived from a great depth of being," but from the surface; and the mark of the collective life is on the individual.

Perhaps our civilization knows how to transform itself; if so, the artist may ultimately have his chance. Perhaps, again, it is permissible to see a kind of allegory in the story of the man who fed his horse on shavings. For some reason, he said, just about as the horse began really to like them, "it up and died on him."

Harper's – September, 1927

*. . . I was sharing the experience of the average
reader; for the vast bulk of popular literature is
no more rewarding than the books I read, and the
attention spent on it must result in the same sense
of futile exhaustion.*

LITERATURE OF ESCAPE

What is one to do with three days and nights in the dry-dock, convalescing from a sudden and venomous indis-position? One might read, if only one had the books and the brains; but the infirmary was short on stuff to read, and I was short on brains. Reading, properly so-called, is an exercise of thought, and my machinery of thought would not run; it was shaky, weak and out of co-ordination. Well, one might pass things through one's mind without thinking about them; one might at least do that — that excellent distinction, by the way, was drawn by Bishop Butler, the great and revered author of the "Analogy." So the "literature of escape" suggested itself at once; the infir-mary had no end of it, and mine seemed to be just the circum-stances for which it was written. I was struck with the thought that I really represented for the moment that elusive person for whom the publishers are always gunning, the "average American reader." I had every qualification: an enervated mind, debilitated nerves, no power of concentration, and an intense desire to be rid of the burden of my circumstances. In short, like the immense majority of my fellow-citizens, I was a made-to-order candidate for anything in the line of a literature of escape, from the *Satur-day Evening Post* up and down.

The nurse brought me two sample volumes of crime and mys-tery; they were done by very competent hands, and provided just the effect they were meant to produce. That is to say, they held my attention to the course of the events they described. Nothing more than that; when I was through with them, I was through;

159

they left no residual impression of any kind, except that I felt the uneasiness of an unrewarded overstrain of attention. I had successfully passed those volumes through my mind without thinking about them or about anything, exercising no intelligence whatever upon the subject-matter of vision. Hence I was more enervated, really, than I had been before, my attention being tired without the exhilaration of having something to show for its exercise. In this, too, I think, I was sharing the experience of the average reader; for the vast bulk of popular literature is no more rewarding than the books I read, and the attention spent on it must result in the same sense of futile exhaustion. I remembered how often, in leafing over popular books and popular magazines — some magazines, too, that are more pretentious — I have thought of Mr. Dooley's experience when he was night watchman on the Canal for two weeks, "with nawthin' to read but th' delinquent tax list and th' upper half iv a weather map."

Presently, however, I got hold of another book, which I should like to mention by name, but in this age of ignorant or unscrupulous book-boosting, one hesitates to do that. I never heard of the author before. His book was a collection of ghost-stories; a modern book, too, published only three years ago, and as far as content goes, quite in the class of escape-literature. Some of the stories had been published in a magazine. Nevertheless the difference between them and the stories I had been reading was just the difference between a hand-made article and a factory-made article, a difference primarily in *intention*. The author was clearly a man of fine culture and large experience, and his intention, first and last, was to produce a story of first-class literary quality. If it met a market, well and good; but whether or not, the quality could not be debased. Hence one could not simply pass it through one's mind; one had to think about it and admire it, and at the end one felt the exhilaration of an abundant reward for one's attention. Probably the greatest piece of artistry ever done in this order is Turgenev's "Phantoms"; and these stories set up, in their degree, somewhat the same sense communicated by that story's unapproachable art. The effect of escape-literature in general — tales of mystery, crime or horror — is produced by sheer content; the effect of Poe's tales, or of these I lately read, or of "Phantoms" or "Clara Militch," is not; and the difference is very great.

Thus I am led up to something that I have already commented on elsewhere, but which will bear a great deal of comment: a peculiar disability that is laid upon the practice of literature in the United States. Americans judge literature only by its content; they do not judge any other art in that way. A painter may paint the corner of a cow barn and be enthusiastically accepted for his workmanship alone. Our people are by no means exacting about the content of music; it is notoriously hard to find out what the program of a concert is going to be; but they are very fastidious, or think they are, about style and finish in its execution. But a creative writer has to furnish content; if he does this, he may pretty well count on his workmanship going unnoticed. If it be good, it will get him no acceptance, and if bad, no reproof. Content is all that is demanded of him. Our reading public, when it reads at all, brings to bear much the same attitude that I assumed towards my escape-literature, and gets about the same results out of it. This being the case, one is sometimes obliged to wonder whether literacy has as much real value as we have been led to suppose it has.

Indeed, my conviction, bred by a fairly broad observation of popular reading-habits, is that a good deal of superstition is mixed into our estimate of the advantages of literacy. Reading, for instance, is supposed to encourage thought, and I can not see that it does. I am not at all sure that a literate population thinks either more or better than one which is illiterate. It may do so, of course, but that it actually does so is doubtful. Everything depends upon what one reads, and upon the attitude taken toward one's reading. It may be quite reasonably doubted, in fact, whether a population like ours, technically literate though it is, is able really to read. Most of those who have come under my observation seem incapable of apprehending an idea conveyed in a sentence of simple prose; they read some prepossession of their own into the sentence, and thus their apprehension is not of what the sentence means, but of what they make it mean. Literacy, again, is supposed to lay open great resources of aesthetic delight, but mostly it does not, for the reasons we have been considering. Most of these resources lie in workmanship, in literary artistry; and where there is no apprehension of this, there can naturally be but little aesthetic pleasure. I can easily imagine most American readers going through "Phantoms" and "Clara Militch," and saying they were fair stuff, a little romantic and pretty thin — not much to them — and nothing to make a fuss over. An analogous criticism would say that Jan Steen's peasants were rather rough-looking birds, not worth a real painter's wasting his time on.

Freeman – February, 1930

It seems to me indeed that the association of plain language with free speech is a natural one; that legality alone is not enough to ensure free speech. Freedom of speech means more than mere freedom under law. It means freedom under a régime of candour and objectivity; freedom under a paramount concern with truth and clearness of statement, rather than a paramount concern with making one's statements acceptable to the whims and sentimentalisms of an enervated people.

FREE SPEECH AND PLAIN LANGUAGE

R ecently, under the title, "So Conceived and So Dedicated," Mr. William F. Russell published an excellent paper,[1] which starts an interesting train of thought. It shows that the author is a true believer in free speech. It ends with an appeal for freedom, which I found most exhilarating; so exhilarating that I at once determined to take it as a text, as I now do. Speaking of the American people's progress in safety and happiness, and of the means to be employed in promoting that progress, Mr. Russell says, "Our only hope is full, free, frank, open discussion from all sides, open propaganda, open influence upon the press, upon public opinion, upon our Congress and legislators, and upon our governors and President. Whoever thinks, let him speak. Whoever would muzzle another, let him stay his hand. Bring on the opposition. Let it be heard. Then shall we have all the forces in full play."

These are noble and inspiring words; well, just what do they mean? I am not asking what they mean to Mr. Russell. I take it that he is a literal-minded person, like the statesman of the last century who said that the way to resume specie payment is to resume. If I might do so without impropriety, I would ask Mr. Russell's permission to place myself beside him in that category. To such as Mr. Russell and myself, then, free speech means simply free speech, whether the words be conveyed by sound or by writing or by printing. That is that, and that is all there is, and there isn't any more — use no hooks. Moreover, it would appear to us

[1] *Atlantic Monthly*, May, 1935.

that the plain provisions of the Bill of Rights mean nothing else, nor can be made to mean anything else, save through one of those processes of interpretation whereby, as a contemporary of Bishop Butler said, anything can be made to mean anything — processes, in other words, of sheer and patent shysterism. But I may remind Mr. Russell that the world seems to be rapidly going away from old-fashioned people of our kind, and it is therefore necessary to consider what free speech means to others who are not like us, and especially to those who are in a position more or less to prescribe the courses in which public sentiment concerning such matters shall run.

A little story occurs to me in this connexion, which I shall tell, partly because it is amusing, but also because it tends somewhat to show what I am driving at.

In the interregnum following the fall of the Tsarist régime, Petersburg was full of spellbinders haranguing the crowds in the public squares, and telling them what they must do to be saved. Some were emissaries of foreign governments. One of my friends was there; he entertained himself all day and every day by wandering around among the crowds with an interpreter, to find out what was going on. In one group that was being addressed in very thick Russian, he found a knot of five or six proletarians, took them aside and questioned them about their odd attitude of docility towards the speaker. "Don't you know that this man is an agent of the German Government?"

"Yes."

"Well, then, he is a dangerous fellow. Why do you listen to him? Why don't you throw him out?"

"Anything the German Government has to say to us, we ought to hear."

This was a stupefying surprise. My friend, being a man of great humour, saw his chance, and went on:

"Is that the way you people generally feel about it?"

"Yes."

"That is your notion of free speech, is it?"

"Yes."

"But you don't seem to know the difference between liberty and license."

"No; what is it?"

"Well, when some perfectly respectable person gets up and says something that everybody agrees to, that is liberty."

They ruminated on this awhile, finally got it down, and then asked, "What is license?"

"Why, license is when some infernal scoundrel, who ought to be hanged anyway, gets up and says something that is true."

The men drew apart and had a long powwow with the interpreter, who finally came forward and said, "These men say there must be some misunderstanding on your part, probably owing to differences in language. They say we are not for liberty at all; we are for license."

I take it that, in the circumstances set forth in Mr. Russell's article, he and I are for license; but the fact remains, I fear, that most of our fellow-citizens are very strong for liberty; very strong indeed.

II

This addiction seems to be the natural fruitage of another addiction which is more or less common to all men, but with us is so inveterate and so ingrained that we might almost take out a process-patent on it; and that is, the addiction to expediency as the supreme law of conduct. Among the many observers who came over from Europe to study us in the early days of our republic, the ablest and most profound was one who for some reason is also most neglected. This was the eminent economist and Saint-Simonian, Michel Chevalier. One never hears of him; yet he is probably worth more to us, especially at the moment, than all the Tocquevilles, Bryces, Chateaubriands and Halls put together. I wish I might prevail on some enterprising editor to arrange with Professor Chinard, who not only knows our history so well but understands it so thoroughly, to write an essay on Chevalier which should bring him out of a most unmerited obscurity and introduce him to us.

Chevalier, who spent four years among us exactly a century ago, traveling everywhere, has a great deal to say about the blind devotion to expediency which he found prevailing throughout our society. He found, in short, that in any circumstances, in any matter small or great, whenever considerations of expediency collided with principle, law, precept or custom, it was invariably the latter that must give way.

Witnessing these collisions, he would ask such questions as, "Where are your principles of action? What about the doctrine set forth in the Declaration of Independence? What about your belief in the natural rights of man?" — and he would get but the one answer, that the action taken in the premises must be regulated by expediency.

Truly, it would seem that Americans of Chevalier's day were temperamentally more ill-fitted for the undertaking of self-government by written statutes, and under a written constitution, than any people who had passed beyond the patriarchal stage of political development. In this very matter of free speech which we are discussing, it is worth remembering that the ink was barely dry on the Bill of Rights when the Sedition Act was passed; and since then the history of free speech in America has pretty well been a history of efforts to show, as Mr. Dooley. said, "that th' Constitution iv th' United States is applicable on'y in such cases as it is applied to on account of its applicability."

So I believe it is unquestionably the inveterate devotion to expediency that has left Mr. Russell and myself standing together in this rather forlorn hope for the future of free speech. It is coercion based on expediency that suppresses what we loosely call "Communist propaganda." It is coercion based on expediency that enforces silence about this or that flagitious transaction in public affairs; and so on. As an abstract issue, free speech comes in for a good deal of discussion now and then, for instance during the late war, when coercion based on expediency was widely applied; and the general run of argument pro and con is probably well enough known. There is one line of argument, however, that is not often brought out. It proceeds from the fact that while, as rule, action based on pure expediency gets the immediate results it aims at, those results always cost a great deal more in the long run than they are worth; and moreover, the most expensive items in the bill are those that were not foreseen and never thought of.

For example, expediency suggested that the evils of the liquor-traffic be suppressed by coercion. It got results, after a fashion, but it got them for us at the price of making corruption and hypocrisy respectable. A heavy price — were they worth it? Again, expediency suggested that the care of our poor be made a government job. It gets results, but at what price? First, the organization of mendicancy and subvention into a permanent political asset. Second, the indoctrination of our whole citizenry with a false and dangerous idea of the State and its functions — that the State is something to be run to in any emergency, trivial or serious, to settle matters out of hand.

This idea encourages, invites, nay, insists upon what Professor Ortega y Gasset rightly calls the gravest danger that today threatens civilization: the absorption of all spontaneous social effort by the State. "When the mass suffers any ill-fortune, or simply feels some strong appetite, its great temptation is that permanent, sure possibility of obtaining everything — without effort, struggle doubt or risk — merely by touching a button and setting the mighty machine in motion."

There is no trouble about seeing how deeply our people are penetrated with this idea; even the cartoons in our newspapers show it. I saw one not so long ago, a caricature of the Revolutionary reveille, the fine old picture that everybody knows, of the old man, his son and grandson, marching three-abreast, with banner, drum, and fife. The cartoon showed three ill-looking adventurers marching on Washington and their banner bore the word, "Gimme."

This degrading enervation of a whole people is rather a heavy offset to the benefits gained through a policy of expediency. The devotees of expediency, however, never consider the final cost of their policies; they are after the immediate thing, and that only. Their case was never better put than by Mr. George Horace Lorimer, in his observations on the young man who pawned a razor for fifteen cents to get a shave.

I had a desultory talk with one devotee of expediency not long ago, a good friend and a thoroughly excellent man. He was all worked up over the activities of Communists and what he called pink Socialists, especially in the colleges and churches. He said they were corrupting the youth, and he was strong for having them coerced into silence. I could not see it that way. I told him it seemed pretty clear that Mr. Jefferson was right when he said that the effect of coercion was "to make one half the people fools and the other half hypocrites, and to support roguery and error all over the earth"; look at Germany and Italy! I thought our youth could manage to bear up under a little corrupting — they always have — and if they were corrupted by Communism, they stood a first-rate chance to get over it, whereas if they grew up fools or hypocrites, they would never get over it.

I added that Mr. Jefferson was right when he said that "it is error alone which needs the support of government; truth can stand by itself." One glance at governments anywhere in the world proves that. Well, then, the surest way to make our youth suspect that there may be something in Communism would be for the government to outlaw it.

"That is all very well for Mr. Jefferson," my friend said, "but think of this: Some years ago an anarchist agitator went up and down the land, preaching the doctrine of terrorism. A weak-minded young man heard it, was unbalanced by it,[2] went forth and shot President McKinley. The State executed him and buried his body in quicklime to show its abhorrence of the deed, but nothing was done about the agitator who provoked it. Is this logical? Lincoln did not think so. When a delegation of liberals complained to him about the Sedition Act, he said, 'Must I shoot a simple-minded soldier-boy who deserts, while I must not touch a hair of the wily agitator who induces him to desert?'"

This is, of course, a sound argument, provided one accept the premise implied. On the other hand, one might suggest that in shooting simple-minded boys and burying lunatics in quicklime, the State is not taking precisely the right way with them under any circumstances. We avoided this digression, however, and returned to the subject in hand.

"McKinley's death was a shocking thing, truly," I said, "but let us try to strike a balance. Don't you think, when all comes to all, that the life of a President, now and then, maybe, — such things seldom happen, — a moderate price for keeping you free of a civilization made up half of fools and half of hypocrites? Men have thought so before now, and pretty good men too. On the occasion of Shays's Rebellion, Mr. Jefferson said, 'If the happiness of the mass of the people can be secured at the expense of a little tempest now and then, or even of a little blood, it will be a precious purchase. *Malo libertatem periculosam quam quietam servitutem.*' Again," I added, "you remember that when Sir Robert Peel proposed to organize a police-force for London, Englishmen said openly that half a dozen throats cut annually in the Whitechapel district was a cheap price to pay for keeping such an instrument of potential tyranny out of the hands of the government.

"That sounds rather cold-blooded, but the immense augmentation and strengthening of the police-forces in all countries in

[2]My friend may have been misinformed. This story was current at the time, but no evidence of it was ever brought forward, and it was probably an invention.

the past fifty years go far to show that they were right. Get up in one of our industrial centres today and say that two and two make four, and if there is any financial interest concerned in maintaining that two and two make five, the police will bash your head in. Then what choice have you, save to degenerate either into a fool or into a hypocrite? And who wants to live in a land of fools and hypocrites?

"Mr. Jefferson was right," I continued. (I could not resist winding up with a little flourish.) "Error is the only thing that needs the backing of government, and when you find the government backing anything you are pretty safe in betting that it is an error. Truth is a very proud old girl, and if you or any crew of ignorant blackguards in public office think she cares two pins for your patronage, or that you can put her in debt to you, you have another guess coming. She will look at your little efforts with an amused eye, perhaps give you one or two mild Bronx cheers, and then when she gets around to it — in her own good time, no hurry, she is never in a hurry — she will stand you on your head. Rome, Moscow and Berlin papers, please copy."

To be on the popular side at the moment is not especially interesting; the thing is to be on the right side in the long run. As I see it, the best argument for free speech is what the suppression of it does to the character of a people. This is the only thing in the whole contention that interests me, though I have every respect for the Bill of Rights. Mr. Jefferson said that "it is the manners and spirit of a people which preserve a republic in vigour. A degeneracy in these is a canker which soon eats to the heart of its laws and constitution." Nothing promotes this degeneracy more effectively than a check on free speech. We all remember, for example, what the "spirit of a people" was like in 1917, when free speech was suppressed, and when any low-minded scoundrel might make character for himself by spying and eavesdropping. The Bill of Rights is all very well, so long as it has the manners and spirit of a people behind it; but when these are hopelessly impaired, it is not worth the paper it was written on.

But, as Mr. Jefferson saw clearly, we can not hope to get something for nothing; and here, I think, is probably the real issue between old-fashioned persons like Mr. Russell and myself, and the believer in expediency like my good and honoured friend whom I have just now cited. My friend unquestionably wants the manners and spirit of our people kept up to par, — it would be a base slander to suggest the contrary, — but when it comes to digging up for it, he boggles at the price; in short, he wants to get something for nothing, and this simply can not be done. The whole order of nature is against it.

I believe I may count on Mr. Russell being with me when I say that, if the spirit of a people is worth maintaining, we must be prepared to accept the offenses, inconveniences and injuries incidental to its maintenance. We must take a chance on terrorists, pink Socialists, Communists and what not; a chance on a fracas or two, on a few youths being corrupted, maybe on losing a President once in a long while, and all the rest of it. Possibly those chances are not quite so desperate as the believer in expediency imagines; I think it very likely. I have a letter just now from a French friend, who says that *quand les Américains se mettent à être nerveux, ils dépassent tout commentaire*; and I too have often thought I noticed something of the kind. However, desperate or not, those chances must be taken.

Julius Cæsar went unattended; he said that life was not worth having at the expense of an ignoble solicitude about it. Considering the outcome, the believer in expediency might say this was quixotic. Yet, on the other hand, it is conceivable that this example was better for the spirit of the Roman people than the spectacle of a *Führer* guarded by squads of secret-service men and plug-uglies. One of the greatest men that England ever produced was Lucius Cary, Viscount Falkland; he was killed in the battle of Newbury, at the age of thirty-three. He held the job of Secretary of State for a year, just when things were warming up nicely for the war. He refused to employ spies or to censor correspondence; he would not open a single private letter. Horace Walpole sneers at this, saying that it "evinced debility of mind." Well, no doubt it incurred the chance of considerable inconvenience, even of some injury; but Falkland seemed to think it better to run that chance, rather than turn loose a swarm of sneaking vermin to deprave the spirit of the people.

So the issue is that "you pays your money and you takes your choice." The believer in expediency appreciates the benefits of freedom, but thinks they are likely to come too high. The old-style doctrinaire, like Mr. Russell and myself, is doubtful that they will come so high as all that, but never mind. Let them cost what they may, he is for them. He is for them unreservedly and unconditionally and world without end.

III

Thought on this subject opens the way for a few words about plain language; and here I must part company with Mr. Russell, for nothing in his article warrants the assumption that he would go with me, though he might — his article intimates nothing either way.

I am thinking particularly about the current treatment of public affairs, though in general I wish we were in the habit of conveying our meanings in plain explicit terms rather than by indirection and by euphemism, as we so regularly do. My point is that habitual indirection in speech supports and stimulates a habit of indirection in thought; and this habit, if not pretty closely watched, runs off into intellectual dishonesty.

The English language is of course against us. Its vocabulary is so large, it is so rich in synonyms, it lends itself so easily and naturally to paraphrase, that one gets up a great facility with indirection almost without knowing it. Our common speech bristles with mere indirect intimations of what we are driving at; and as for euphemisms, they have so far corrupted our vernacular as to afflict us with a chronic, mawkish and self-conscious sentimentalism which violently resents the plain English name of the realities that these euphemisms intimate. This is bad; the upshot of our willingness to accept a reality, provided we do not hear it named, or provided we ourselves are not obliged to name it, leads us to accept many realities that we ought not to accept. It leads to many and serious moral misjudgments of both facts and persons; in other words, it leads straight into a profound intellectual dishonesty.

The glossary of business has many such euphemisms; for example, when you hear that a concern is being "reorganized," it means that the concern is bankrupt, unable or unwilling to meet its bills; it is busted. "Bankruptcy" has, however, become an unfashionable word; we are squeamish and queasy and nasty-nice about using it or hearing it used. We prefer to fall back on the euphemism of "reorganization."

The glossary of politics is so full of euphemistic words and phrases — as in the nature of things it must be — that one would suppose politicians must sometimes strain their wits to coin them. For example, when Secretary A. tells Congressman B. that unless he votes right on a certain measure there will be no more pork-barrel funds distributed in his district, that is blackmail, — there is no other name for it, — but we prefer to lump off transactions of this sort under the general and euphemistic term "Patronage." Sometimes we find a euphemism on a euphemism; for example, what we used to call an indemnity is what our ruder ancestors called booty, plunder, which is precisely what it is. But the word "indemnity" became in turn unfashionable, for some reason, — overwork, perhaps, — and for the last few years we have been saying "reparations." Some literary artist spread himself to give us "unemployment relief," when it became evident that the good and sound word "dole" was a little heavy for our pampered stomachs; and while we all know well enough what "mandated" territory is, and what "mandates" are, we are quite indisposed to saying what they are, or to hearing anyone say what they are.

A person never sees so clearly how absurd these euphemisms are until he translates a few of them from another language into his own. The French language has a small vocabulary, and its genius is rather against euphemism, — as much against it as English is for it, — but it can turn out a few very handsome ones. Embezzlement, for instance, is known as an "indelicacy"; you will read in French newspapers that yesterday's cashier who made off with the contents of the safe "committed an indelicacy." Italian newspapers, reporting a bad accident on the railway, will begin by telling you that the Sunrise Express "disgraced itself" yesterday morning, at such-and-such time and place; casualties, so-and-so many. These sound as ridiculous to us as our pet euphemisms must sound to a Frenchman or an Italian; the reason being that all such sophistications of speech are intrinsically ridiculous. They sound silly because they are silly; and, being silly, they are debilitating.

Bad as euphemism is, however, indirection is worse. I notice that a writer in a recent magazine gives this advice to budding newspaper men:

> Even where opinion is admitted, as on the editorial page, fact is often more desirable than opinion. Thus it is better to scrap an editorial calling the mayor a liar and a crook, and to write another which, by reciting facts without using adjectives and without calling names, makes it obvious that the mayor is a liar and a crook.

In the view of journalism, that is first-class good advice, because we are all so accustomed to indirection that a lapse from it affects us unpleasantly and sets us against the person or organ that indulges in any such lapse; and that will not do for journalism, because it makes people stop their subscriptions.

In the view of intellectual integrity, on the other hand, this advice seems to me about the worst imaginable. In the first place, if the mayor is a liar and a crook, saying so is certainly "reciting facts." It is not calling names," it is not uttering abuse or vituperation; it is a simple and objective recital of fact, and only a weak and sticky supersensitiveness prevents our seeing it as such. In the second place, indirection is so regularly the vehicle of propaganda that the use of it marks the man with an axe to grind. The advice which I have just cited contemplates a person who is more concerned with producing an effect on people's minds than he is with the simple expression of truth and fact. This may be good journalism, — I am not entitled to an opinion about that, — but I can find nothing to say for it on general grounds.

After the jury in the Beecher-Tilton trial disagreed, and the case against Beecher had lapsed, Charles Anderson Dana said editorially in the New York *Sun*, "Henry Ward Beecher is an adulterer, a perjurer, and a fraud; and his great genius and his Christian pretenses only make his sins the more horrible and revolting." To me that piece of plain language sounds purely objective. On the one hand, it has not the accent of mere vituperation, it is thoroughly dignified; and on the other, it is not the language of a person who is mainly concerned with wangling somebody into believing something. When Mr. Jefferson wrote that one of his associates in Washington's cabinet was "a fool and a blabber," his words, taken in their context, make exactly the same impression of calm, disinterested and objective appraisal as if he had remarked that the man had black hair and brown eyes.

Or again, while we are about it, let us examine the most extreme example of this sort of thing that I have so far found in English literature, which is Kent's opinion of Oswald, in *King Lear:*

> *Kent.* Fellow, I know thee.
> *Osw.* What dost thou know me for?
> *Kent.* A knave; a rascal; an eater of broken meats; a base, proud, shallow, beggarly, three-suited, hundred-pound, filthy, worsted-stocking knave; a lily-livered, action-taking whoreson, glass-gazing, & super-servicable, finical rogue; one-trunk-inheriting slave; one that wouldst be a bawd, in way of good service, and art nothing but the composition of a knave, beggar, coward, pandar, and the son and heir of a mongrel bitch.

Now, considering Kent's character and conduct, as shown throughout the play, I doubt very much that those lines should be taken as merely so much indecent blackguarding. I appeal to Mr. Walter Hampden to say whether I am not right in thinking that an actor who ranted through them in the tone and accent of sheer violent diatribe would ruin his part. Frank Warrin cited those lines the other day, when he was telling me how much he would enjoy a revival of *Lear*, with our gifted friend Bill Parke cast for the part of Kent. He said, "Can't you hear Bill's voice growing quieter and quieter, colder and colder, deadlier and deadlier, all the way through that passage?" Angry as Kent is, and plain as his language is, his tone and manner must carry a strong suggestion of objectivity in order to keep fully up to the dramatist's conception of his rôle. Kent is not abusing Oswald; he is merely, as we say, "telling him."

IV

I repeat that I have no thought of weaving a web of implications to entangle Mr. Russell. I may say, however, how greatly I wish he would go at least some little way with me in the belief that, with the revival of free speech which he so ably urges, there should go a revival of plain language.

When we speak freely, let us speak plainly, for plain speech is wholesome; especially, plain speech about public affairs and public men. Mr. Justice McReynolds gave us a noble specimen of it in his dissenting opinion and his accompanying remarks on the gold-clause decision. Such language has not been heard from the Supreme Bench since the days when John Marshall Harlan used to chew up about half a pound of plug tobacco, just "to get a good ready," and then turn loose on his affirming associates with a dissenting opinion that would burn a hole through a rawhide. Nothing like it, indeed, has been heard from any public man in America, as far as I know, since the death of William Jay Gaynor; and it bucked me up almost to the point of believing that there might be some sort of future for the country, after all.

That is the sort of talk we should be hearing on all sides of any and every public question, and with reference to every public man. I have long since given up reading political editorials and the "interpretations" of political reporters. I detest a flavoured stink; and the stench of propaganda that has been soaked in the musk and patchouli of indirection is peculiarly odious. If these interpreters set out, say, to deal with some public man of rank and responsibility who is on the other side of the political fence, they usually begin by buttering up his good intentions, fine gifts and excellent character, and then proceed to associate him with some flagrant piece of political rascality; thus by indirection making it appear that he is actually a knave and a dog. Really, one loses patience with this perpetual and exclusive concern with making people believe something, with "putting something over," rather than with plain objective statement. Even the editorial technique of Mr. Pott and Mr. Slurk had at least the merit of eschewing indirection.

It seems to me indeed that the association of plain language with free speech is a natural one; that legality alone is not enough to ensure free speech. Freedom of speech means more than mere freedom under law. It means freedom under a régime of candour and objectivity; freedom under a paramount concern with truth and clearness of statement, rather than a paramount concern with making one's statements acceptable to the whims and sentimentalisms of an enervated people.

This thought tempts me to go on and examine some specific infringements on the relation between freedom of speech and plainness of language; it brings Jeremy Bentham back to mind, with his chapter on what he calls "impostor-terms." But this essay is already too long, and I must end it here. If my reader's patience holds out, I may take the matter up again and carry it on from where I now leave it.

Brussels, July, 1935
Atlantic Monthly – January, 1936

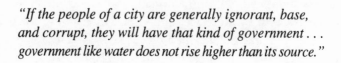

"If the people of a city are generally ignorant, base, and corrupt, they will have that kind of government . . . government like water does not rise higher than its source."

— William Jay Gaynor, 1848 – 1913

NEW YORK'S JEFFERSONIAN MAYOR

William Jay Gaynor died twenty years ago, and twenty years is a long time for a man's memory to last. When the mayoralty of New York was so much in the public eye lately, I thought it would be a good time to see whether any one remembered him. I tried out five candidates; a corporation lawyer from Wall Street, a Southern editor, a mid-Western politician, and a business man and a young doctor, both of the latter New Englanders. I got the same response from all of them, in practically the same words.

What struck me particularly was how prompt they were in lighting up at my mention of his name. "Gaynor was a great man," said the lawyer, in a tone of real reverence, "a great lawyer, and a great man." The editor said, "I have believed for years that he was the best man ever heard of in public office in America." "He stood by himself" said the doctor. "There has never been one like him in our later public life." Perhaps among our millions I happened to hit on the only five who remembered him in this way, but even that is something in these days.

As an American executive, Gaynor seems to me to stand alone, for he actually *did* what we *say* — what we say on the Fourth of July, what spellbinders talk about at election time in the rural districts. He actually carried out what we call the American idea of the function of a public servant under democracy. To begin with, when he became mayor, he laid down the fundamental principle set forth in the Massachusetts Bill of Rights, that government in America is a government of laws and not of men, and he never lost an occasion, great or small, for hammering that principle into the public mind. He had not been long in office before the so-called moral element in New York went on the warpath against the exhibition of prize-fights in moving pictures. A clergyman wrote to Gaynor, asking him to suppress these exhibitions, and the return mail put this flea in his ear:

> Will you be so good as to remember that ours is a government of laws, and not of men? Will you please get that well into your head? I am not able to do as I like as mayor. I must take the law just as it is, and you may be absolutely certain that I shall not take the law into my own hands. You say you are glad to see that the mayors of many cities have "ordered" that those pictures shall not be exhibited. Indeed! Who set them up as autocrats? If there be some valid law giving any mayor any such power, then he can exercise it; otherwise, not. The growing exercise of arbitrary power in this country by those put in office would be far more dangerous and is far more to be dreaded than certain other vices that we all wish to minimize or be rid of. People little know what they are doing when they try to encourage officials to resort to arbitrary power.

One of the fine specimens of that unctuous rectitude in which for some reason our unhappy country seems to specialize, wrote to Gaynor for advice. He had been elected justice of the peace in Oak Park Ill., and was in doubt about the ethics assessing fines for petty offenses, as by law provided, and also about the ethics of collecting his own fees. Gaynor replied:

> You ask if Jesus would assess such fines and collect such fees if He were in your place. You seem to be a man who thinks himself wiser and better than the law, and above the law. That kind of man is most dangerous that can be put into office, especially in a free country. . . . Suppose every judge in the country, from the highest to the lowest, took it into his head to ignore the law and decide cases to suit himself. What a woeful condition that would very soon put us all in! And yet you, a little justice of the peace out in Oak Park, Illinois,

want to act in that way! As to your fees, neither Jesus nor any one else cares whether you collect them or not.

In 1912 the Superintendent of Public Instruction asked Gaynor for a message to be read to all the school-children of New York on the Fourth of July. He got it. Not a scream from the eagle, not a word of fustian about the Founding Fathers, or about how grand and glorious our civilization is, how good and wise we all are, and above all, how rich. Instead, about 800 words of a magnificent exposition of what republican government really is, and what the people's responsibility for it is — sound, old-fashioned American doctrine, mostly in words of one syllable. It ended with this:

> We must therefore be vigilant of every little approach to despotism, however little it may be. We must see to it that those whom we elect to office do not go outside of the laws, or set themselves up above the laws, and do as they please. It has always been the case throughout the world that the officials who did this did it on the plea that the laws were not good enough; that they could do better than the laws prescribed. Beware of all such officials. We do not want officials who have any lust of power. We want officials who are very careful about exercising power. We want officials who are careful to exercise no power except that given to them by the people by their laws. There is no more dangerous man in a free country, in a democracy, than an official who thinks he is better than the laws. The good man in office should be most careful not to set a bad example or precedent for his bad successor, who will come along sooner or later.

Perhaps Gaynor's unfailing example of staunch law-abiding did some good; perhaps his masterly expositions of it did some good. Yet it is a humiliating reflection for an American, that if he had lived only four years longer, he would have seen at Washington just such an administration as he held up for the detestation of those school-children; an administration led by just such men as he declared most dangerous — and such men acting at their very worst.

183

One must wonder sometimes what would have happened if Gaynor had been the Democratic nominee in 1912, instead of Wilson. He was supposed to be headed that way, via the mayoralty and the governorship, and at one time was regarded as the best vote-getter the Democrats had. But he would not take the governorship in 1910, and in declining it he also put his foot hard down on the Presidential idea. "I am not a candidate for Governor, and cannot be made a candidate," he wrote. "As for myself or my political future, I shall not consider that at all. Mr. Watterson is in error in supposing that I have the Presidency in mind. Never!"

It is not a matter of record that Gaynor ever said anything that he did not mean, or (which is far more remarkable) that he ever meant anything that he did not say. But if he had been President, and had lived out his term, we would have seen no such doings as we did see in that trying period. Old-fashioned believers might think the Lord put it into Gaynor's heart to feel that way toward the Presidency, because as a nation we needed chastening. I am not sure they would be wrong; at any rate, we got the chastening, and we got it good and hard.

II

Another sterling old American principle (or so at least we call it when our patriotism is on dress-parade) is that "the only way to enforce the law is the way prescribed by law." The words are Gaynor's own, but he did not invent the principle, although many citizens of New York seemed to think he did, judging by their surprise when he announced it. One man of wealth and prominence told him it would be impossible to cope with crime on any such principle as that, and Gaynor crisply replied, "Then don't."

Twenty years ago, the moral element was very busy making life as disagreeable as possible all round, and naturally it fell foul of moving pictures, in which great multitudes were beginning to find pleasure. New York's moral element badgered the Board of

Aldermen into passing an ordinance creating a censorship, and Gaynor promptly vetoed it. In his message he said that the law governing such exhibitions was clear and sufficient, and that the way to enforce it was the way prescribed by the law itself. He cited the State and Federal Constitutions as plainly providing that "publications, whether oral or printed or by writing or by pictures, shall not be restrained in advance, but that every one shall be free to speak and publish what he sees fit, subject to being prosecuted afterward for libel, immorality, obscenity or indecency therefor." If any one published anything contrary to law, he should be punished for it, but the law was against advance judgment on the part of any one. This ended the matter, except for a rap at the motives of the people who wanted a censorship. The movies, he said, were attended largely by those who could not afford to pay theatre-prices.

> Why are we singling out these people as subjects necessary to be protected by a censorship? Are they any more in need of protection by censorship than the rest of the community? That was once the view which prevailed in government, and there are some among us, ignorant of, or untaught by, past ages, who are of that view now. Are they better than the rest of us, or worse?

But what most disturbed and perplexed the right-thinking citizens of New York was his enforcement of this principle on the police. He stopped the practice of making arrests without warrant and without evidence of crime. In a sharp letter to the police commissioner concerning the illegal arrest of an eighteen-year-old boy, he said:

> The police must be made to understand that they cannot arrest and lock people up as they like, but that they must keep within the law. The only way to enforce the law is the way prescribed by law. That which cannot be done lawfully must not be done at all, by the police or any other public officials, from the President of the United States down. This is a government of laws and not of men.

This was news to New York, where, as Gaynor said, "all over the city decent people had been clubbed, mistreated and insulted for years." By doing away with petty, unneccssary and blackmailing arrests, he cut down the total of arrests by over 100,000 a year. Incidentally, this destroyed the business of the professional bondsmen, whose habit was to split their fees with the policemen who made the arrests. In a preface to the police manual for 1912, he told the police to remember that "your chief business is to keep outward order and decency, and arrest real criminals, not good citizens guilty only of some small thing." People so little knew what to make of this that "outward order and decency" was for some time a phrase in everybody's mouth.

He stopped the practice of photographing arrested persons before conviction. He did away with the so-called special police, of whom there were about 1300 in New York. These were men sworn in as policemen, thereby becoming public officers, and then turned over to the pay and orders of private persons and firms. He also stopped the police from taking sides in strikes and labor disputes, thereby drying up a source of graft — one officer who was disciplined for this offence got as much as $1000 from an employer.

In dealing with corruption in the force, he took the method of separating the police from the sources of graft. He took away from the general police force all supervision over saloons, gambling-houses and houses of prostitution, and created a special force for the purpose, placing it under the immediate orders of the commissioner himself. This was the best he could do under certain sections of the city charter, of which he said, "No better device for the practice of official extortion and blackmail could be devised than that afforded by these two sections." Nevertheless, his method worked well, reducing corruption until "it was never less in the police department for a generation than during the past two years."

He stopped entirely the practice of forcible entry, visitation and inspection of private premises, at will and without a warrant. "It is always easy," he explained in his message to the Board of Aldermen, "to get a warrant from a magistrate to enter a house when necessary. If no evidence can be found to lay before a magistrate on oath, that in itself shows that the house should not be entered."

III

Another good old American doctrine which he followed faithfully is that no public man or institution is wise enough or good enough to put himself or itself above criticism. In Gaynor's time, Socialism was not as well understood as it is now, and people were more nervous about it. A Socialist meeting in Union Square usually got the same sort of attention from the police and the public that Communist meetings get nowadays. In a message to the Board of Aldermen, Gaynor laid down the law on this point:

> I have particularly made the police authorities understand that those who entertain views of government, or of economic or social order, different from ours, are not to be interfered with or denied the right of freedom of speech and of assembly on that account. A propaganda by intellectual persuasion and peaceable means for changes in form of government or in the economic or social order, is lawful, and not to be meddled with, much less oppressed, by the police. The Socialists do not believe in individualism, but in collectivism [here followed a precise statement of Socialist doctrine] . . . That it clearly appears to the rest of us that this scheme would, by doing away with incentives to individual exertion, greatly reduce production and thereby increase poverty and distress, is no reason for denying to those who advocate it rights secured to every one by our system of government.

Gaynor always had a great horror of any menace to the rights of free speech and free assembly, even the menace implied by the mere presence of policemen. Two weeks after he took office, in a letter to one of his department heads, he laid down the principle that "we must not only deal with people with justice, but also with the appearance of justice, the latter sometimes being as essential as the former." He knew that people did not like to see policemen around their meetings, because it implied that they were not going to behave themselves, or else did not know how to behave peaceably and properly. Gaynor sympathized with their resentment. In a speech in 1912, reported in all the papers, he told the public exactly what they might expect, and why they might expect it:

> There is a notion abroad that you people need policemen to keep you in order. When we have a political meeting, people think they must have an army of police there. Now, I did something this year that will make you laugh, because nobody knew about it. It was given out in the paper that a Bull Moose meeting up at Madison Square Garden was to be policed by 1000 policemen. Didn't you read that? Hearst put it in his paper, so it must be true. I had already instructed the police commissioner [Waldo] to stop sending policemen to political meetings, except large meetings that might need protection on the outside. It used to be the fashion to have them inside at meetings like this, and at weddings and funerals.
>
> Now, I asked Waldo how many he was going to have at the Bull Moose meeting. "Well," he said, "I guess about 100." I said, "Waldo, cut it down to fifty." And there were just fifty policemen at that meeting. They were all on the outside, and we didn't allow one to go in the inside at all. . . . And then the Wilson meeting was coming on, so I said to Waldo, "I have a notion to have no policemen go there." He said, "Well, the others had fifty, and maybe this year we ought to give them fifty." So I said, "All right, let the fifty go." But the next time we will keep quiet and send nobody at all and see what happens. Now I have let the cat out of the bag, so that if you have a big meeting here next year, maybe there will be no policemen at all, and those people who read what I am saying tonight will certainly be writing me letters to send police to keep the people from killing one another.

Gaynor himself was free enough in his criticism of men and institutions. He had none of the politician's pliancy and was never on the fence. I have read a great many of his judicial opinions, messages and letters, and never yet found one sentence that was slippery, ambiguous or hesitant The pernicious of freemasonry jobholding meant nothing to him.

He was sixteen years on the bench of the State's highest court; yet I do not know of a hotter grilling that the Supreme Court of the United States ever received than the one he gave it before the Yale Forum in 1912. He took as his text the four famous, or infamous "due process of law" decisions, and his treatment of what is known as the Bakeries Case may serve as a sample of his critical approach. After describing the underground bake-oven as "the hottest and most uncomfortable place on earth," and easily made one of the most unsanitary, he spoke of the law that the Supreme Court had declared unconstitutional:

> One of the regulations was that ten hours a night was all that a baker should work in those places. To do credit to our State courts, they said it was a reasonable law, that it was a fair health law, and they approved of it. But it got up to the Supreme Court of the United States in some way, and that court, by a vote of five to four, as is usual in important matters, decided that the act was unconstitutional and void because it deprived the journeyman bakers of the liberty of working all night in bake-ovens if they wanted to. That is exactly the decision. They said it took away their liberty. There were no journeyman bakers that I know of clamoring for any such liberty . . .
>
> Judge Peckham [who wrote the opinion] said for the court that the question was whether it [the act] was a fair and reasonable exercise of legislative power. And he said no, it was not. But who is the judge of that, pray? Who made him the judge of it, pray? Who made any court in the land the judge of that, against your will? If you, by which I mean the intelligent people of any State, conclude that it is a fair and reasonable thing to limit the hours of work in these bake-ovens to ten hours in one night, if enlightened public sen-

timent comes to that conclusion, I want to know where any court in this land was given the power to set that enlightened public sentiment at naught and overthrow it.

No wonder New Yorkers rubbed their eyes over their newspapers every morning in those days, and wondered what things down in the City Hall were coming to, for no officeholder since Thomas Jefferson had ever taken that tone toward the Supreme Court; and not Thomas Jefferson himself ever lodged a more vigorous protest against judicial usurpation than this which followed on the foregoing. After defining the "police power" of the legislature, he said:

> But, say the courts, we will keep the decision to ourselves whether a given statute is fairly and reasonably for the "health, comfort, morals, safety, or general welfare." It is not enough that the Legislature and those who elected it think so and say so. The Legislature may debate it. They may collect statistics on it. Benevolent people may work upon it. The law may be passed unanimously by the Legislature and signed by the Governor and meet the wishes of the whole State. But we, we, mind you — or I, if it happen to be one judge — reserve to ourselves or to myself — big I and little you — the question whether it is such as is reasonable and fair and necessary or not. All I say is that we have given no such power to the courts.

But while criticism should be as free and forceful as you like, it must come after the fact, and never before. It is good Americanism again, that if you leave a thing to a responsible officer, you leave it to him. After he has acted on it, you are free to say exactly what you think, but not before. In the same speech Gaynor gave out this canon of criticism to the young men of the Yale Law School very definitely:

> Never let any one get it out of your mind that the judges are public officials just like mayors and Governors, like myself and Governor Baldwin, and open to public criticism just as we are, neither more nor less. We can not criticize them while they have a case before them. Ordinary decency re-

quires that we remain mute — not like some newspapers, which tell them how to decide it, and do the whole thing for them. We have to keep still until they have made their decision. But as soon as they make it we have a right to discuss it and criticize it if we want to, and pick it to pieces if we can.

IV

Another principle which Gaynor always exemplified is one that we would all like to think is American if the facts were not so ludicrously against any such idea. That is the principle of ordinary common sense — horse sense — in legislation.

American lawmaking has for generations been a mere riot of ignorance and fantastic foolery, which has burdened us with an array of statutes that omnipotence could not enforce, and that no one in his right mind would want enforced. Gaynor set himself against this on every occasion, sometimes by learned and serious exposition in his messages and speeches, and also very often in his letters by his favorite device of answering a fool according to his folly; which indeed never does any good to the fool, but may set wiser persons to thinking. He put the principle seriously, but with a nice touch of irony, to the Politics Club of Columbia University:

> We very often think (and that is one of the falsest notions in politics) that we can cure ills by passing laws. Not so. The distance between the passing of a law and its observance is often immeasurable. No law is worth anything unless it is backed up by the community, and even then you have hard work to get it enforced. The Ten Commandments are not too well observed, so far, are they? And yet they are backed up by the community and by all the preachers.

A specimen of his epistolary method is seen in his reply to a reformer who got on a high horse about prostitution, and urged the system of segregation. Gaynor answered:

> How would you do it? It is very easy to mark off a district by law or ordinance, but how would you get the women to

go there and stay there? Will you undertake the job to catch them and bring them into that district? And after you get them there, who will keep them there? . . And you ask whether the women should not be inspected. How could you find them to inspect them? If there were a law for such inspections, how many out of the whole number would come forward for inspection, and if they did not come forward, how do you think they could be found? . . . It is easy to pass laws and ordinances, and to talk, and say this ought to be so and that ought to be so, but the doing of it is another thing. No law should be passed which is not enforceable.

One more principle of old-fashioned Americanism is that the office should seek the man, not the man the office. Gaynor seems never to have shown any ambition for more than a plain citizen's part in politics. He twice declined nominations that would have made him Governor (the one in 1910 leading straight to the Presidency), twice the mayoralty of New York, and once the mayoralty of Brooklyn. He even declined the judgeship which he afterward accepted under strong pressure; but once in it, he seemed to think it suited him, and he remained there. It must be clear, I think, that his attitude toward public office was consistently American. What man who was thinking about votes or nominations would ever put anything like this into a public speech that he knew would be reported next day by every paper in New York?

Every time I go to Albany or to Washington I cannot help looking at the people around, not only some of the legislators, but the people who come there. Did you ever see such a lot of gabby people, and so many sharpers, and so many small people? And they look so cagey, did you ever notice? I was over in Washington recently, and that was the one thing I said to the man that was with me, "Let's get away from here. I never saw so many cagey-looking people." At the Capitol, even at the White House, in the outer room, and especially in the lobby of the hotels — every man a gabby, cagey little fellow.

Or this, with reference to two mighty men in the moral element that was almost all-powerful in the country in Gaynor's time, and is still potent enough to make jobseekers prayerfully cautious:

> I thank you for the good will of your letter. You advise me to "pay no attention to Dr. Parkhurst" and harsh people like him. When did I ever pay any attention to him or them, or even to the Rev. Rabbi Wise, except now and then to say a jovial word or two about them to make them feel good? . . . To think oneself good, or better than others, is a mental trait which is hard to overcome by those who are afflicted with it. It is even reckoned a disease among physicians, and has a name. That is an additional reason why we should forbear and overlook. And you know there are people who think they are pious when they are only bilious.

I think a fair and reasonable test of Gaynor's disinterestedness toward public office would be to imagine Mr. Hoover or Mr. Roosevelt adopting this tone toward two great masses of political power, at any time these last seven or eight years.

V

These five points of sterling Americanism take up all my space, so that I can not speak of Gaynor on the side of his learning, culture, humor, his range of interest and knowledge, or his sound and prophetic sense of fundamental economics. I hear that a biography of him has been published lately, which presumably deals with these matters, but I have not seen it. I hope it is a good one, for he should be made the subject of a really great biography.

My experience with the five people I mentioned at the beginning encourages me to give my own opinion, which I have held for more than twenty years, that Gaynor was the greatest man, taken all round, that has appeared in our public life since Mr. Jefferson, and also the soundest American. Hence I think a really great literary treatment of him would take rank with the world's standard books — it would be a classic. The trouble is that America seems to have gone entirely away from people of Gaynor's kind, so I suppose not many would read it.

Gaynor is said to have had faults of temper. One of his associates at the City Hall told me that sometimes "you pretty well had to feed him off the end of a pole." But he said also that the things Gaynor was impatient with were the sort that any one with any character ought to be impatient with, and that in all other circumstances Gaynor was always reasonable and equable; and for all I ever heard to the contrary, this is true.

He made a grand lot of enemies, but in the retrospect of twenty years they seem to be the sort of people that one would do one's level best to keep clear of, whether in this world or in the next. Gaynor had nothing in common with the saponaceous political liberalism that was rife in his period. Messiahship, too, was out of his line. He seems also to have had a bitter hatred of pretentiousness and showmanship, especially when it took the guise of civic virtue. Hence as time has sifted and weighed the men who were his enemies, one may say that they do him credit

Life in New York under Gaynor was pretty interesting — interesting and stimulating. I had a good sample, and I know. One felt that something might really come of it, that it had at least a dog's chance to become reasonably enlightened and civilized. One felt that certain essential integrities were displacing bogus platitudes, that self-respect and dignity had some sort of place in civic life. *Civis Romanus sum* seemed to be on its way to mean something. A decent citizen did not have to be all the time squirming around to keep on the windward side of himself. He could hold his head up, and that is an agreeable sensation.

One cannot have it now.

American Mercury – December, 1932
Entitled: Notes On A Great American

In relation to business, the proper functions of government are three, and no more. First, to punish fraud. Second, to enforce the obligations of contract. Third, to make justice costless . . . But would our businessmen wish to be told that? I think I have reason to doubt it.

BUSINESS DODGES THE TRUTH

My personal doings are very seldom important enough to be worth anybody's notice, but I have lately had an experience which I think might interest some of my readers, so I shall take a chance on describing it.

First, though, I shall ask the reader to look at an imaginary picture. Suppose you saw a country where people were tremendously interested in Christianity, all giving themselves out to be sound, hundred-per-cent Chrisitians, and then suppose you found that in the whole length and breadth of that country you could not buy a copy of the New Testament for love or money. What would you think?

Suppose further that you went around among publishers in that country, and said, "This is a queer kettle of fish. How about getting out a cheap edition of the New Testament just as a flyer, and see what could be done with it. I can't believe but that these people would want to have a copy around the house for the looks of the thing, if nothing more" — and the publishers all told you it would be a dead loss, that nobody would buy it if you offered it in paper covers as low as twenty-five cents.

Still further, suppose you then looked up some rich men who were especially strong on Christianity, not only in a personal way, but officially — vestrymen, deacons, trustees, elders, and all that sort of thing — and who were all terribly worried because Christianity was being cold-shouldered by a godless government just then, and they didn't know what to do about it. Suppose you suggested that they might buy up a small edition of the New

Testament and distribute it around among influential people as ammunition, with a strong personal letter accompanying each copy. The letter would say that in this time of trouble Chrisitians who were really up-and-coming ought to know something about the first principles of their faith, its history and general philosophy; that the New Testament was a pretty fundamental document in those respects, and no Christian who expected to be called on to defend his faith could afford to leave it unread. Then suppose these men told you that they did not know of anyone who would read it as a gift, or who would let it go any further with him than the nearest waste-basket!

I imagine you might think there must be a screw loose with Christianity in those parts, and that the sooner the godless government made hay of it, the better.

I have lately been dabbling in a noble experiment of that kind, with results pretty much as stated. When I arrived in this country after a long absence, I found that our great captains of industry were in a terrible twitter over the government's interferences with business. They were saying that the government ought to get out of business, keep its hands off business, let business alone. I was immensely pleased to hear this, because it was exactly what I had been saying for a great many years. I was a good bit astonished, too, for I had never heard businessmen talk that way before, and whenever I had ventured to talk that way, I had found myself distinctly unpopular. Nevertheless I was glad to see myself in good company at last, and so I started in at once on the best move I could think of to help the cause of righteousness along.

For anyone who really wants the government to let business alone, Herbert Spencer's essays called *The Man Versus the State* are precisely what the New Testament is for anyone who wants to be a sound intelligent Christian. They are *the* fundamental document, an impregnable arsenal, bristling with irresistible philosophical and historical weapons. A businessman who is framed up with this volume knows just where he stands and what the real strength of his position is, and he knows how to defend that position against all comers. It is a small book, too. In England, if you don't mind taking it in a paper cover, you can buy it for an English shilling, somewhat under twenty-five cents. In this country, unless you have the luck to pick up a second-hand copy somewhere, it is not to be had.

Well, then, like Mr. Squeers with the milk, I said to myself, here's richness. Here is something which will at last put me really solid with my newly-made friends, and maybe give me a chance to die in the odor of respectability. Businessmen will jump at it. They will see that we old-fashioned radical individualists whom they have so long sneered at and despised were actually on their side all the time and were the best friends and defenders they ever had, as in fact we were. They will see that the old horse-and-buggy fellows like Franklin, Paine, Thomas Jefferson, Quesnay, Herbert Spencer, Henry George, Turgôt, du Pont de Nemours, had something on the ball; and that the disciples of these men, like myself, were not quite the cranks and crack-pots we were taken for, but had the businessman's best interests steadfastly at heart.

I have quite a few acquaintances in the publishing business, some of them pretty enterprising, so I went around among them, suggesting that since our businessmen were so het up about governmental interferences — and most justly — it might be worthwhile to republish Spencer's essays. I even offered to do the editing, free gratis for nothing. The publishers looked at me with a pained expression; they were pleasant and friendly but evasive. They quickly shifted the conversation with a few well-chosen words, and I saw it was useless to pursue the subject further.[1]

---

[1]Publisher's Note: It is interesting to note that Nock, ever the gentleman with an impecable sense of what he would call manners, promoted the reprinting of Spencer's *The Man Versus The State*, for which he had written the introduction, rather than his own recent in-print work, *Our Enemy, The State*.

That didn't work. I then looked up some acquaintances who are close to various eminent captains of industry, and suggested that one or another of these captains take a cheap edition of Spencer and send it around to a picked list of representative businessmen throughout the country, with a personal letter. This did not work either. I was told that the representative businessmen would not read the book, could not be hired to read it, and that the eminent captain of industry who was fathering the issue would not read it himself; so that was that.

My last attempt of this kind was especially interesting. The person I talked with was on very close terms with the heads of an immense concern — something in the mining way, I think. He was sympathetic and extraordinarily frank. "This talk of wanting the government to let business alone," he said, "is all hooey. They don't want it to let business alone. Go to them today and offer to set up a government tomorrow on Spencer's model, one that would really let business alone, and they would die in hysterics. What! — no tariffs, no 'protection', no subsidies, franchises, concessions, nobody to run to when you get into a jam over some competitive scheme to swindle somebody? Do you think they would stand for that? Show them how to make a clean sweep of Roosevelt and John Lewis, and they'll give you their daughter in marriage, or all their daughters if you want 'em, and you can take 'em tandem, four-in-hand, or six-abreast. But show them how to put a crimp forever in *all* the Roosevelts and Lewises, their own kind included, and see what you'll get. Take it from me, the last thing they want is to abolish privilege, precisely as it is the last thing John Lewis wants. They want to *monopolize* privilege, which, is just what Lewis wants, and your friend Spencer would stand the same show with them as he would with Lewis or with Roosevelt himself, and not a dam' bit better."

II

To tell-the truth, I had more than half suspected something of this kind. My newspaper this morning carried an item about a whaling big new subsidy granted to a shipping firm. It started up in my mind once more the question of who ever got the government into business, anyway. Who got it into the shipping business? Politicians? I'm afraid not. The reader probably knows by this time what I think of politicians — at least, as much of it as can be put into print in a family magazine — and that I would never give one of them an out unless it were unmistakably coming to him. To my mind, the American jobholder, from poundmaster to President, is the very lowest form of verminous life. To his credit be it said, however, that he tried hard to keep the government's hands off the shipping business; he fought ship-subsidies for years. It was a nice little junta of businessmen — shipbuilders, steelmakers, outfitters, and such — who put the government in the shipping business, and thereby created one of the most notorious rascal-nests in the country. Have these men undergone a change of heart lately so that they now want the government to let the shipping business alone? Not according to this morning's newspaper.

The papers also say that the railways are hard up and must have some relief from the government. Well, who nagged the government into the railway business, cadging land-grants and subsidies in the first instance, and then running to Washington for political rate-fixing and regulation of traffic? Who pestered the government into the aviation business, the road-building business, the business of dredging harbors and worming out internal waterways? Who hectored the government into setting up things like the Federal Trade Commission and the erstwhile Farm Board? Businessmen, every time. Just so; and now do businessmen want the government to take its hands off those businesses and forever after let them alone? I don't believe it.

But I am not in the least interested in merely showing up the American captain of industry as a Bourbon and a humbug. That is a poor thing to do, and gets nowhere. What interests me is the impressive evidence now before us that there is no practicable middle ground, or No-Man's Land, between a type of government which lets business strictly alone to hoe its own row, and the type which dabbles progressively in all business, as ours is now doing, and thereby runs society down into a most calamitous bust. There is no such thing as successfully segregating certain areas of business activity in which it is proper for the government to take a hand, and others in which it is not. Letting one group use the government to promote a group-interest or class-interest means letting any and all groups use it, according as one or another, by fair means or foul, can get itself a break.

My point is, then, that either you take Turgôt, Franklin, Spencer and Co., and take them straight, or in the long run you get chaos. At the present time our society has yet but a short way to go before landing in chaos, and there is no chance but it will keep going. That is the upshot of a century-and-a-half of feverish wangling for breaks by economic group-interests and class-interests. Once admit that there are any breaks to be had, no matter how few, no matter how sharply de-limited, and the government immediately becomes an auctioneer.

In relation to business, the proper functions of government are three, and no more. First, to punish fraud. Second, to enforce the obligations of contract. Third, to make justice costless. If anyone wishes to know why this is so and why no society which adds one jot or tittle to these functions can permanently hold together, Spencer will tell him in terms which no one can misunderstand or fail to understand. But would our businessmen wish to be told that? I think I have reason to doubt it.

American Mercury – November, 1938

The first of these is called the law of diminishing returns, the second is called Gresham's law, and the third one is so seldom cited that it has no pocket-title . . . "man tends always to satisfy his needs and desires with the least possible exertion."

THE GODS' LOOKOUT

Not long ago I glanced at a book called *Natural Law in the Spiritual World*, which had a great vogue in its time, half a century, ago. Having never read it, I had a moment's curiosity to find out why it was so popular. I did not get far with it, because I saw at once that it dealt mostly with "great matters which are too high for me," and, like the Psalmist, I was diffident about meddling with them. The title, however, served to precipitate a notion which had been vaguely in my mind for some time, that, whatever may be the case in the spiritual world, certain laws and principles have a wider application in the material world than they are commonly supposed to have. I had been thinking in particular of three laws that are officially recognized in economics, but I believe nowhere else, and it seemed to me that they operate about as regularly and powerfully outside this restricted sphere as they do inside it. The first of these is called the law of diminishing returns, the second is called Gresham's law, and the third one is so seldom cited that it has no pocket-title. I shall say a word about the first two now, and consider the third later.

The law of diminishing returns is fundamental to industry. It formulates the fact, which strikes one as curiously unnatural, that, when a business has reached a certain point of development, returns begin to decrease, and they keep on decreasing as further development proceeds. Thus I suppose, according to the logic of the deacon's one-hoss shay, it is theoretically possible for a business to be so big that it would not bring in any returns at all. I know nothing of such matters, having never been in business, but I am told on good authority that the law of diminishing returns is much more effective than the antitrust laws for protecting society against the oppression of industrial monopoly. The idea is that when a business becomes overgrown and returns decrease, small independent concerns can begin to compete profitably, eating in around the edges of the big concern, and meanwhile reaping the fruit of the big concern's labours in developing the market.

Gresham's law has to do with the nature of currency, and the common formula for it is that "bad money drives out good." That is to say, it is always the worst form of currency in circulation that fixes the value of all the others, and causes them presently to disappear. This law bears the name of Sir Thomas Gresham, an eminent English financier of the sixteenth century, who made observations on the law, but was not the first to formulate it. Gresham's law usually comes into play whenever a government undertakes to settle a bill for its misfeasances by the larcenous expedient of "managing" its currency; hence of late years this law has been very busy with the currency of many countries. In Germany, for example, shortly after the war, the flood of paper money sent all metallic money out of circulation in a hurry, because it was worth more as old metal than as currency. For the same reason, whenever a paper or silver token is no longer the same thing as a gold token, gold tokens disappear at once; and then, if a government resorts to highwaymanry and forcibly robs its subjects of whatever gold may be in their possession, as our government lately did, it can do quite nicely by itself.

The Belgian Government raided its currency after the war, cutting down the franc from twenty cents to three cents and less, and the mint began putting out an odd-looking sort of one-franc piece that seemed to be made of tin. A few days after this, a man gave me a pre-war silver franc as a curiosity; he had got it somewhere in change. I have never seen another. As far as I know, silver francs have not been demonetized or confiscated, — certainly they were not at that time, — but I doubt whether there were half a dozen of them in circulation in all Belgium a week after the tin franc appeared.

II

The term "natural law" is a pocket form of expression, handy enough, but inexact and easily lending itself to improper assumptions. As a matter of fact, what we call a natural law is nothing more than a registration of experience. If human experience of some natural phenomenon has been uniform, it sets up a correspondingly strong expectation that subsequent experience will be likewise uniform, and we call the formula for that experience a natural law, even though the term be a misnomer, strictly speaking, for we actually know of no "law" anywhere in the universe that guarantees the fulfillment of our expectation. It is always with this understanding — or it should always be — that one speaks of the laws of optics, the law of gravitation, Huyghens's law, and so on, as "natural laws"; and thus likewise when one speaks of Gresham's law and the law of diminishing returns.

Mr. James Truslow Adams and others have commented on the social incidence of the law of diminishing returns, so we need give only two or three illustrations showing how this law works in the realm of æsthetics and culture. There is a whimsical saying current among music-lovers that the way really to enjoy the music of a string quartette is to have the performers group themselves around your chair. This is no great exaggeration. Let us suppose that a string quartette plays the *Kaiserquartett* to an audience of five qualified amateurs in a music-room of ordinary size. The five get a distinct æsthetic experience in a high degree, probably the highest of which they are capable. It is the nearest thing to a sense of actual participation. Logically, if five get this, forty should get it in the same degree, so next evening they ask in as many amateurs as the room will hold comfortably, say thirty-five, the strings play the *Kaiserquartett* again, but the thirty-five do not have the same experience to the same degree, nor do the original five have it. Next evening the strings play the *Kaiserquartett* to three hundred qualified amateurs in a public hall, and while all hands get something very interesting, pleasant, delightful, nobody gets just *that*. It is simply not there to be had; it is gone.

We all remember how our tourists used to plume themselves on the nice little places they had found in Europe, "where nobody ever goes," and we may remember, too, that we were sometimes tempted to put this kind of talk down to snobbishness. Far be it from me to suggest that snobbishness is not an inveterate trait in our nation, but I think that in this instance our tourists are entitled to a clean bill. I think instinct warned them that a great influx of qualified seekers after an æsthetic experience similar to theirs would carry their own experience over the margin of diminishing returns; and their instinct was sound, for that is precisely what it would do.

I spent a month last summer on an island in the Mediterranean, a small one, difficult of access, and almost uninhabited. It has great natural beauty, but no doubt other islands have as much. Its peculiar charm is in the sentimental associations created by an unbroken run of rich and fascinating history which reaches far back beyond the Christian era. Hence, from the time of Nostradamus and Rabelais down to the present, men of letters have sung this island's praises, poets and romancers have found in it an abundant source of inspiration. The few qualified persons who go there have an experience so rewarding that I know of none of the same kind to compare with it. Suppose now that other persons, persons well furnished with the rather special qualifications necessary for the purpose — suppose that they heard of this experience, assumed that because a few had it any number might have it, and began to flock thither in large droves: the æsthetic returns would promptly decrease, and not only would the many fail to get precisely this experience, but the few would no longer get it. Nobody would get it. Instances where this has actually occurred will suggest themselves at once, for they are many.

We may take one more illustration, this time recalling the old and sound definition of a university as a student sitting on one end of a log and Mark Hopkins on the other. One may assume that the student was a qualified person, for otherwise Mark Hopkins would not be sitting there; he would have got up and gone home. That student got a specific return, peculiar to just those circumstances. Suppose now that twenty qualified persons notice this, think it is a good thing, go in for it; well, they too get pretty much the same thing in the same degree, but probably not quite. Hopkins is still there, the log is still there, but the margin of diminishing returns is close at hand. Then a hundred come in, three hundred, five hundred, only to discover that the margin was crossed somewhere far back in the beginning of the stampede, and that nobody is getting anything like what the original student got, or even the next twenty.

In the foregoing illustrations I have been careful to premise that all the persons cited are qualified. The listeners to the concert, the visitors to the island, and Mark Hopkins's students, are all supposed to be qualified in intellect, character, temperament, and a certain degree of preparatory experience, to take in and assimilate whatever benefit the several occasions may offer. I do this to show what happens when the law of diminishing returns works "straight" and without any complications; in other words, to show what happens on the theory so commonly held, that if a few qualified persons get a certain benefit, any number of qualified persons may get the same benefit under the same circumstances.

If, now, we substitute the theory which is much more widely held, that if a few qualified persons get this benefit, anybody, qualified or unqualified, may get it, we may perceive at once, I think, that the margin of diminishing returns would move considerably forward; also that the more unqualified persons tend to predominate, the further forward it would move. Going back to our illustrations, the larger the proportion of unqualified persons among the concert-audience, the visitors, and the students, the sooner the law of diminishing returns would set in. This is a matter of such common experience that it needs no comment, so we will pass on to consider the appearance of a second "natural law" in the premises.

III

Suppose the concert-audience of three hundred or more were made up largely of casual and miscellaneous persons; the natural thing for the musicians to do would be to change their programme. They would not play the *Kaiserquartett*; they would play something that they thought would hit nearer to a common denominator of their audience's capacities. In fact, it occurs to me at the moment — I had not thought of it before — that I have never seen the *Kaiserquartett* on an American programme; which of course is by no means to say that it has never appeared on one. It is a mere commonplace that programme-making for a qualified audience is one thing, and that for a popular audience it is quite another; and this is true because popular programme-making finds itself always striving against the iron force of the law that "bad money drives out good." One might doubt that Mr. Kreisler, let us say, makes up his programmes out of the kind of thing that he would choose to listen to himself. Programme-making like Mr. Damrosch's, for example, does its best to slow down the operation of Gresham's law, but even Mr. Stock's, to name the best we have in the way of programme-making, shows that it can not be successfully withstood. The development of the gramophone and the radio has encouraged the notion that by keeping a great deal of poor music in circulation one creates a larger demand for good music and helps a taste for good music to prevail. But we are discovering that things do not go that way; and the reason is that a "natural law" is moving them in a direction exactly opposite.

The current repertory of the radio shows this, quite as the current repertory of the cinema shows the same law at work in the field of drama. The radio enables Mr. Damrosch to pick up eligible persons, one by one, all over the country, and offer them advantages which they would otherwise be unlikely to get. The gramophone performs a like service, and it is a very great one. But the stated repertories of both instruments are evidence of the continual tendency of an enormous volume of indifferent music to press upon Mr. Damrosch and crowd him out; they, like the repertory of the cinema, are an impressive study in the operation of Gresham's law. It is the worst music in circulation, and the worst motion-pictures, that fix the value of all the others, and continually tend to drive them out.

By way of example in another field, two or three recent experiences have made me wish that some competent person like my friend Mr. Duffus would undertake a study of literacy in the light of Gresham's law and the law of diminishing returns. Not long ago I looked over a library said to contain a copy of every book published in America down to the year 1800. It bore witness that in those days reading was a fairly serious business; I could find nothing resembling what we should call popular literature on the shelves. The inference was that literacy was not general, and that those who read did so for other purposes than mere pastime, purposes that were pretty strictly non-sensational; and there is every collateral evidence that such was the case.

Mr. Jefferson laid great stress on literacy as an indispensable asset to good citizenship and sound patriotism. He was all for having everybody become literate, and those who have examined his own library (it is preserved intact in the Library of Congress) may easily see why. *Mutatis mutandis*, if everybody read the kind of thing he did, and as he did, he would have been right. But in his laudable wish to make the benefits of literacy accessible to all, Mr. Jefferson did not see that he had the operation of two natural laws dead against him. He seems to have jumped to the conclusion that, because certain qualified persons got a definite benefit out of literacy, anybody could get the same benefit on the same terms; and here he collided with the law of diminishing returns.

He seems also to have imagined that a general indiscriminate literacy would be compatible with keeping up something like the proportion that he saw existing between good literature and bad; and here the great and good old man ran hard aground on Gresham's law.

I spent some time last year in Portugal, where the status of literacy and the conditions of the book-market are about what they were in Mr. Jefferson's America. One saw very little "popular literature" on sale, but an astonishingly large assortment of the better kind. I made my observations at the right moment, apparently, because, like all good modern republicans, the Portuguese have lately become infected with Mr. Jefferson's ideas about literacy, and are trying to have everybody taught to read and write; and it interested me to see that are setting about this quite in our own incurious, hand-over-head fashion, without betraying the faintest notion that anything like a natural law may be a factor in the situation.

Doubtless what has happened elsewhere will happen there. In the first place, the Portuguese are likely to discover that, while no illiterate person can read, it is a mere *non distributio medii* to conclude that any literate person can read. The fact is that relatively few literate persons can read; the proportion appears to be quite small. I do not mean to say that the majority are unable to read intelligently — I mean that they are unable to read at all — unable, that is, to gather from a printed paragraph anything like a correct idea of its content.[1] They can pretty regularly make out

---

[1] In the interest of accuracy, I submitted these statements to a prominent educator who says that his experience fully bears them out. He carried on experiments over a dozen years with college freshmen — that is to say, with persons who were not only literate but had gone so far as to pass their entrance examinations. He experimented in this way: selecting a paragraph of very simple but non-sensational prose, he asked the freshmen to read it carefully; then to read it carefully again; then to read it aloud to him; then to write down in their own words the gist of what they had read. Hardly anyone could

the meaning of printed matter which is addressed to mere sensation, like newsmatter, statistics, or perhaps an "informative" editorial or article, provided it be dosed out in very short sentences and three-line paragraphs; but this is not reading, and the ability to do it but barely implies the exercise of any faculty that could be called distinctively human. One can almost imagine an intelligent anthropoid trained to do it about as well and to about as good purpose; in fact, I once heard of a horse that was trained do it in a small way. Reading, as distinguished from this kind of proficiency, implies a use of the reflective faculty, and not many persons have this faculty. According to the newspapers, Mr. Butler, the president of Columbia University, was complaining the other day that the practice of reflective thought had pretty well ceased among us. There is much to be said on this topic, but it is enough to remark here that literacy will not do duty for the power of reflective thought where such does not exist, nor does a state of literacy presuppose its existence.

To cite a rather comical illustration of this truth, a clerical friend lately told me of the troubles that a candidate for confirmation was having with the Nicene Creed. This candidate was a man of more than middle age, completely literate, and of considerable prominence and wealth. The article that he balked at, curiously, was non-theological and non-metaphysical; it was the one which sets forth that the Saviour "was crucified also for us under Pontius Pilate." He wanted to know why they crucified Pontius Pilate. He knew who Pilate was, and what his rôle was in

---

do it. He made the interesting remark that the reflective faculty is more easily stirred by speech than by print, because the communication of ideas by hearing is an older racial practice; their communication by sight is something comparatively new, to which the race's capacities are not as yet well adjusted. Therefore, he said, the indiscriminate spread of literacy puts into people's hands an instrument which very few can use, but which everyone supposes himself fully able to use; and this, obviously, is mischievous.

the great drama, but he had never before heard anything about Pilate's being crucified, and he wondered why the circumstance should be brought in here as one of those things which a Christian should know and believe to his soul's health.

A person of any literary experience, even the slightest, sees such instances time and again, not usually so bizarre perhaps, but essentially quite the same — instances which show beyond peradventure that the persons concerned simply can not read. When confronted with a paragraph requiring the most moderate exercise of reflective thought, they are helpless; and no equipment of sheer literacy can possibly make them less helpless. I have published so little and in such desultory fashion that I can claim nothing for my own experience with the public; yet I regularly get letters from persons who have manifestly gone as far with my writings as literacy will carry them, but who are as manifestly unable to make out correctly the content of English prose as simple and direct as the prose I am writing now.

As for the operation of Gresham's law, one need say little; it is so easily discerned that a glance at the nearest news-stand will show it well enough. The average literate person being devoid of reflective power but capable of sensation, his literacy creates a demand for a large volume of printed matter addressed to sensation; and this form of literature, being the worst in circulation, fixes the value of all the rest and tends to drive it out. In this country, for example, it has been interesting to see the reluctant and gradual submission of some of our few "serious" publications to this inevitable fixing of value. They have brought their aim continually closer to the aim of journalism, addressing themselves more and more to sensation, less and less to reflection, until now their policy favours almost exclusively the kind of thing one would naturally look for in an enterprising Sunday newspaper. Only the other day I came across a market-letter put out by a firm of literary agents, and I observed with interest that "the serious essay, travel, foreign-affairs type of article is unlikely to find a good market, unless by a well-known name."

I had occasion lately to look up something that one of our "quality" magazines published in 1874, and as I went through the two bound volumes I noticed the relative space they gave to material addressed to the power of reflective thought. For curiosity I made a comparison with last year's issues of the same magazine; and I can not suggest a more convincing exercise for any person who doubts the validity of Gresham's law in the premises, nor can I suggest a more substantial basis for generalization.

Gresham's law has, in fact, done far more than revolutionize publishing; it has set up a brand-new business. In the face of this fact, which seems none too well understood, we see publishers and authors occasionally showing something of the splendid intrepidity that one admires in the leader of a forlorn hope, and one thinks of them as perhaps the most public-spirited of all created beings. A little while ago my friend Mr. Van Loon, for example, who is a very learned man, brought out a superb book, quite the kind of book that he himself would be glad to read; one need say no more for it than that. He and his publisher must both have known that they could not turn a penny by it; if it paid for itself it would be lucky. The full force of Gresham's law was pressing them instead to put their time and money into another of Mr. Van Loon's ingenious and attractive vulgarizations of history, which would be "sure fire" with a large literate public; yet they went on — went on in the teeth of the fact that under Gresham's law a "good book" must be a book as much as possible like another book that has sold a great number of copies.

What I have been driving at in all this is the suggestion that if we must reëxamine our social theories we should do so with an eye to natural law. Everyone seems a little uneasy about these theories at the moment, and many of our leading publicists say that they must be overhauled; well, if that be so, the practical thing would be to keep on the lee side of natural law while we do it. We have been a little careless about this hitherto, and the consequences are suggestive. Our idea of mass-education, for example, does vast credit to our intentions; like perpetual motion, the thing would be fine if it would work, but the mischief of it is to keep it from colliding with natural law. As results stand now, a graduating class of two, three or five hundred persons is practically nothing but a tableau-display of what the law of diminishing returns can do when it tries. Again, the promotion of mass-literacy is a noble experiment, but apparently there is no way to accommodate our idea of it to the insidious action of Gresham's law. With regard to these and all other aspects of our equalitarian social theory, my only aim is the humble one of suggesting that we bear in mind the disregard that nature has for unintelligent good intentions, and the vixenish severity with which she treats them.

IV

Finally, since various aspects of political theory are much to the fore just now, I suggest that we follow the same procedure with regard to them. Our ideas about the function of government may be very praiseworthy, very creditable, but surely the first thing is to find out whether natural law is with them or against them; and it is in this connexion that I cite the third law which I mentioned at the outset. This law is fundamental to economics, though for some reason our professional economists seldom say much about it; its formula is, *Man tends always to satisfy his needs and desires with the least possible exertion.* Not, it must be understood, that he always *does* so satisfy them, for other considerations — principle, convention, fear, superstition or what not — may supervene; but he always *tends* to satisfy them with the least possible exertion, and, in the absence of a stronger motive, will always do so.

A candid examination will show, I think, that this law is also fundamental to any serious study of politics. So long as the State stands as an impersonal mechanism which can confer an economic advantage at the mere touch of a button, men will seek by all sorts of ways to get at the button, because law-made property is acquired with less exertion than labour-made property. It is easier to push the button and get some form of State-created monopoly like a land-title, a tariff, concession or franchise, and pocket the proceeds, than it is to accumulate the same amount by work. Thus a political theory that admits any positive intervention by the State upon the individual has always this natural law to reckon with.

At the time our government was set up, a century and a half ago, some political thinkers, notably Franklin, had perceived the incidence of this law. Their idea was that it should be no function of the State to intervene upon society's economic life in a positive way, but only negatively as occasion required, to punish fraud and to safeguard the general régime of contract.[2] Aside from this, the State's only function should be that of safeguarding the lives and liberties of its citizens.

Contemporary British liberalism had the same idea; it advocated a rigid policy of State abstention. Liberalism's career was remarkable in presenting a most instructive object-lesson to those who study it in the light of natural law. Its programme missed one point, admitted one exception; and the consequences of this imperfection forced liberalism in the end to turn squarely around on its basic principle, and become godfather to the most elaborate series of positive interventions ever conceived in England.

This imperfect policy of non-intervention, or *laissez-faire*, led straight to a most hideous and dreadful economic exploitation; starvation wages, slum-dwelling, killing hours, pauperism, coffin-

---

[2]Franklin wrote, "Perhaps in general it would be better if government meddled no farther with trade than to protect it and let it take its course. Most of the statutes or acts, edicts, *arrêts* and placarts of parliaments, princes and States, for regulating, directing or restraining of trade, have, we think, been either political blunders or jobs obtained by artful men for private advantage, under pretense of public good." *Works*, vol. II, p. 401.

ships, child-labour — nothing like it had ever been seen in modern times. Mr. Gradgrind, Mr. Bottles and Mr. Plugson of Undershot worked their will unhindered with a fine code of liberalist social philosophy behind them, and the mess they made shortly stank in the nostrils of all Christendom. People began to say, perhaps naturally, if this is what state abstention comes to, let us have some State intervention.

But the State *had* intervened; that was the whole trouble. The State had established one monopoly, — the landlord's monopoly of economic rent, — thereby shutting off great hordes of people from free access to the only source of human subsistence, and driving them into the factories to work for whatever Mr. Gradgrind and Mr. Bottles chose to give them. The land of England, while by no means nearly all *actually* occupied, was all *legally* occupied; and this State-created monopoly enabled landlords to satisfy their needs and desires with little exertion or none, but it also removed the land from competition with industry in the labour-market, thus creating a huge, constant and exigent labour-surplus.[3]

Franklin saw this clearly; he used Turgôt's language almost word for word to show that the "labour-problem," *qua* labour-problem, really does not exist — it is purely a problem of State intervention, State-created monopoly. He said:

> Manufactures are founded in poverty. It is the number
> of poor without land in a country, and who must work for
> others at low wages or starve, that enables undertakers [i.e.,
> enterprisers] to carry on a manufacture . . . But no man who
> can have a piece of land of his own, sufficient by his labour
> to subsist his family in plenty is poor enough to be a manu-
> facturer and work for a master.

But liberalism did not see this, never saw it; and the consequence was that in the end it was forced by political necessity to

---

[3]Publisher's Note: Vast grants of land by the Crown to loyalists created land monopolies. However, to this date, vested interests have not allowed a pure market economy (laissêz-faire) to flurish in any modern State.

sponsor an ever-lengthening, ever-widening programme of regulations, supervisions, exemptions, subsidies, pensions — every measure of positive State interference, almost, that one could think of.

When the State has granted one privilege, its character as a purveyor of privilege is permanently established, and natural law does not permit it to stop with the creation of one privilege, but forces it to go on creating others. Once admit a single positive intervention "to help business," as our euphemism goes, and one class or group after another will accumulate political power in order to command further interventions; and these interventions will persist in force and frequency until they culminate in a policy of pure Statism — a policy which in turn culminates in the decay and disappearance of the society that invokes it.

Such is the grim testimony borne by the history of six civilizations, now vanished, to the validity of the law that *man tends always to satisfy his needs and desires with the least possible exertion.* We ought to be quite clear about this, as a matter of understanding the course of our present governmental policy. Some of us incline to regard the New Deal as something out of the run of our national history and unrelated to it, whereas it is exactly what the run of our history must inevitably have led up to.

One need only shift a switch in the New York Central's yard some three inches to determine whether a train shall go to Boston or to Chicago. We shifted the switch a hundred and fifty years ago, and set the national train toward the Chicago of hundred-per-cent Statism, with our old friend natural law furnishing abundant steam. The New Deal means merely, that we are now somewhere near South Bend, Indiana, and going strong; and if anyone knows how to reverse that train and head it toward Boston without an awful catastrophe, he is just the man that a good many of us would like to see.

The American State at the outset took took over the British principle of giving landlords a monopoly of economic rent. That

shifted the switch; it established the State's character as a purveyor of privilege. Then financial speculators sought a privilege,
and Hamilton, with his "corrupt squadron in Congress," as Mr.
Jefferson called them, arranged it. Then bankers, then industrial-
ists; Hamilton also arranged that. Then, as the century, went on,
innumerable industrial subgroups, and subclasses of special interest, were heard from, and were accommodated. Then farmers,
artisans, ex-soldiers, promoters of public utilities, began to accumulate political power with a view to privilege. Now, since the
advent of universal suffrage, we are seeing the curious spectacle
of the "unemployed" automatically transformed into the stron-
gest kind of pressure-group; their numerical strength and consequent voting-power compelled Mr. Roosevelt to embrace the extraordinary doctrine that the State owes its citizens a living — an
expedient little noticed at the time, I believe, but profoundly
interesting to the student of historical continuity.

Moreover, as we saw in the case of Mr. Bottles and Mr. Plugson
of Undershot, when the State confers a privilege, natural law
impels the beneficiary to work it for all it is worth; and therefore
the State must at once initiate a whole series of positive interventions to safeguard, control and regulate that privilege. A steady
grist of "social" legislation must be ground; bureaus, boards and
commissions must be set up, each with its elaborate mechanism;
and thus bureaucracy comes into being. As the distribution of
privilege goes on, the spawning of these regulatory and supervisory agencies also goes on; and the result is a continuous en-
hancement of State power and a progressive weakening of social
power, until, as in Rome after the Antonines, social power is
quite extinguished — the individual lives, moves, and has his
being only for the governmental machine, and society exists only
in the service of the State. Meanwhile, at every step in this process, natural law is pushing interested persons, groups and fac-
tions on to get clandestine control of these supervisory agencies
and use them for their own advantage; and thus a rapid general

corruption sets in, for which no cure has ever yet been found, and from which no recovery has ever yet been made.

V

In a sense, no doubt, it seems officious to write a paper that squints toward a vindication of natural law, because natural law is quite competent and handy at vindicating itself; it needs no help, and has no notion of being any man's debtor. Tiberius Cæsar said in his strong common sense way that "offenses against the gods are the gods' lookout," and perhaps it would be as well, certainly less thankless, if one should leave in their hands such little matters as those I have been discussing. Indeed, one must do that finally, for one can not hope that criticism based on nothing more pretentious than the plain natural truth of things will be much regarded; so probably as much or as little would be gained by doing it in the first instance.

Yet, in another view, it may be worth while to point out to simple-minded persons like myself, who are perhaps a little confused by the outpourings of publicists and the din of eager innovators, that natural law still exists and is still a respectable force. I have read many words about social reconstruction, industrial reconstruction, political reconstruction; in fact, as I write this paper I am inspired by the latest efforts in the great new enterprise of "economic planning." All these, in their innocent disregard of natural law, remind me of a piece of music I once saw, written for a cornetist. The music was good, but the composer had not put in any rests for the cornetist to take breath; well, as soon as one saw that, one knew that further examination of the piece was pointless. So, in what the journalists call "these hectic days," a suggestion that natural law is still at work, and that there is really not much that one can do about it, may be somewhat of a time-saver and trouble-saver to minds of the simpler sort, like my own; and to such, and such only, I offer it.

New York, February, 1934
Atlantic Monthly – June, 1934

"*Albert Jay Nock's* Mr. Jefferson, *is a superb biographical essay, beautifully written and penetrating in analysis; Mr. Nock understands Jefferson so well that one despairs of going at all beyond him.*"

Richard Hofstadter
Columbia University

ISBN 0-87319-024-6
224 pages, Trade Paper, $12.95

Gems of Nock's thought, selected from 14 of his books by Robert Thornton and arranged by subject matter.

ISBN 0-87319-039-4
128 pages, Trade Paper, $6.95